It is the second day since the Jeesh al-Mahdi (JAM) attacked Sadr City in one of the biggest offensives in years. The Iraqi battalion executive officer (my current Iraqi counterpart) is dead, shot in the back of the head at one of the checkpoints in Sadr City. My anxiety level is as high as I can ever remember. My thoughts are clouded with the strange dreams (more like nightmares) and restless sleep from multiple nights of listening to barrages of incoming and outgoing mortars, artillery, and rockets firing. The battalion S2 from the Iraqi battalion stops at our building at 3:00 am to inform us that JAM elements are attacking the perimeter. The buzz of multiple large-caliber automatic weapons in the distance confirms his report. Exactly two weeks are left until we redeploy. Our replacements are on the ground in Iraq, but they cannot get to us because all the helicopters are being diverted in direct support of combat operations. I wonder aloud to myself, is this all just a really long, bad dream? If so, how do I wake myself up? Pinching myself hurts. This must be real.

—From *Dreams of Hope*

A Transition Team's Adventures in the Iraq War

Dreams of Hope

Greg Grossman

Cover art by Stephen Adams

authorHOUSE®

AuthorHouse™
1663 Liberty Drive
Bloomington, IN 47403
www.authorhouse.com
Phone: 1-800-839-8640

First published by AuthorHouse 7/30/2010

ISBN: 978-1-4343-9872-7 (e)
ISBN: 978-1-4343-9871-0 (sc)

Library of Congress Control Number: 2010908238

Printed in the United States of America
Bloomington, Indiana

This book is printed on acid-free paper.

For my wife and children

The views expressed in this work are solely those of the author and do not represent the views of the Department of Defense, the Department of the Army, or any other branch of the U.S. government. The situations presented are based loosely upon actual events, but certain details and names of individuals are changed or omitted to prevent harm to individuals serving in Iraq today.

Contents

Preface

It was an e-mail conversation with my sister that made me think I should really write this book. Our conversation was something like this: "Sis, you wouldn't believe the things I have seen over here already. I've only been here for four months, and I've seen more crazy stuff than I can remember in my entire army career." My sister said, "Write a book." So I did.

Illustrations

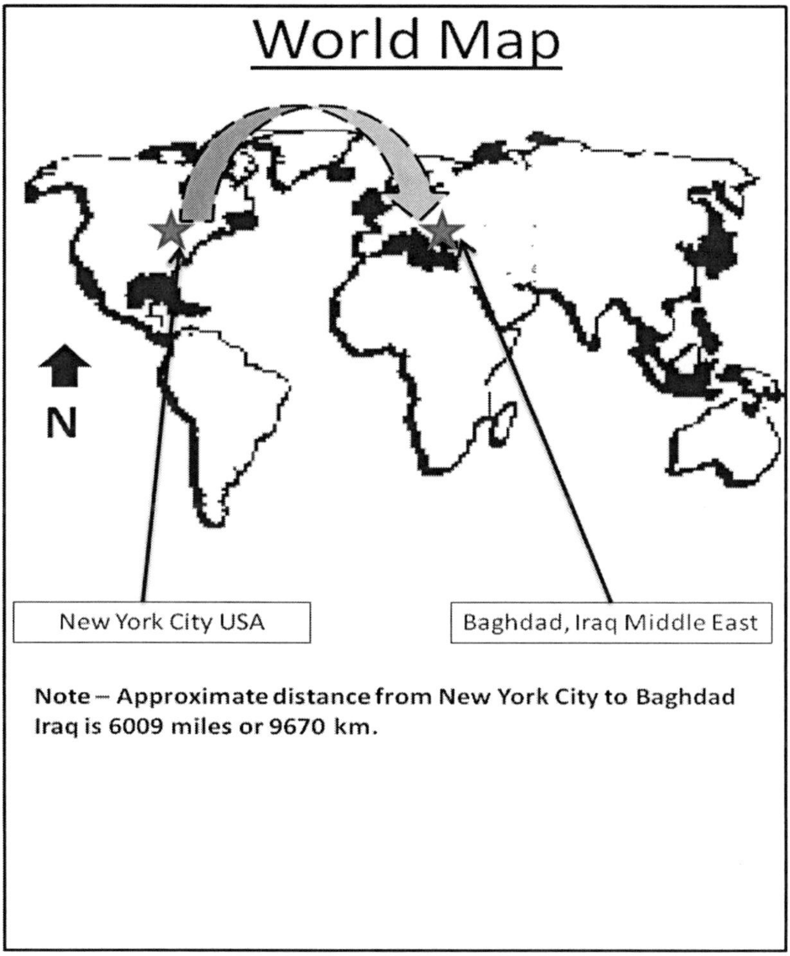

Map by Gregory W Grossman

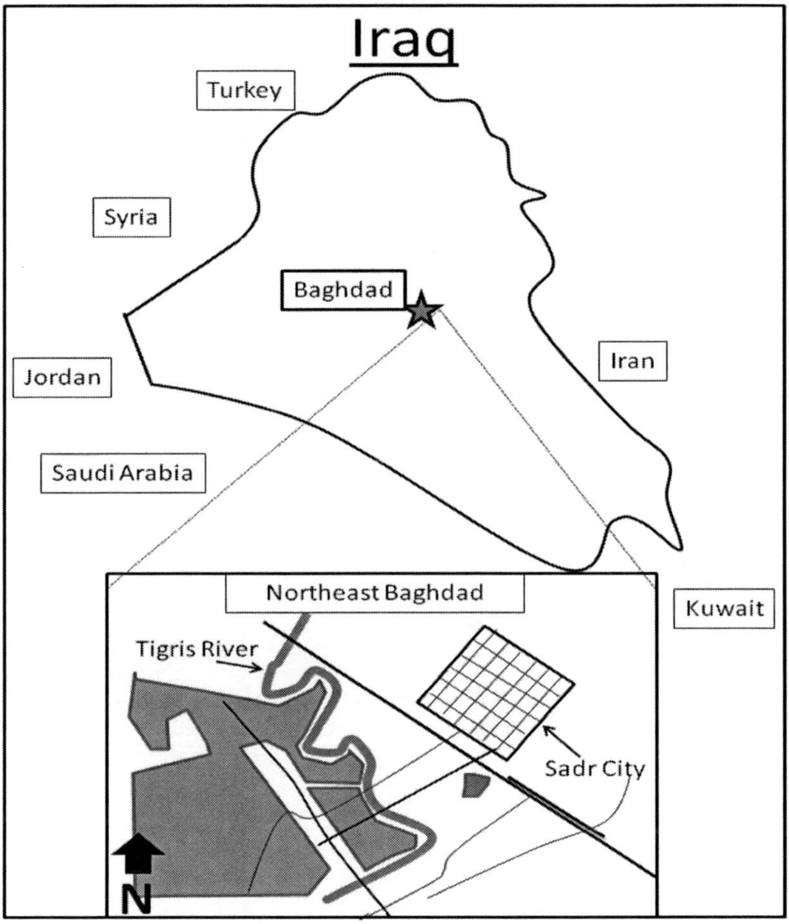

Map by Gregory W Grossman

Major Characters

Author's Note: I have given real persons fictitious names and changed certain details to protect them. "Naming," labeling with an apt nickname, is a common practice in military units and teams. Some funny mistake made by the person being named usually becomes the focus of their new moniker, and some of our own team names are included.

Strongarm—Major Ima Strongarm is the team leader of the transition team and the officer-in-charge in most of the situations. His sense of humor is considered a little weird. Someone who had a bad joke told about them was referred to by team members as having been "Stronged." He has many bosses and difficult tasks, and he has to balance this with the hodgepodge of team member personalities to make things work. Strongarm is a tall guy with a tour in Kosovo under his belt. His wife is pregnant when the story begins, and he is looking forward to seeing his first child when he goes home on leave.

Calderon—Also referred to as "Tapeworm," Master Sergeant Jimmy Calderon is the senior noncommissioned officer (enlisted rank E8) assisting Major Strongarm and supervising the enlisted personnel on the team. A red-headed firecracker is the best way to describe him. Calderon is a smart, short-tempered Irish fellow who has the not-so-easy task of keeping the team working well together and accomplishing the majority of the team's business. He is a veteran of Panama and Operation Iraqi Freedom.

Z—Captain Doug Zabilinski is the operations officer for the team. He keeps track of the team missions, writes operations and movement orders, and trains the Iraqis on various classes. A veteran of Operation Enduring Freedom in Afghanistan and Operation Iraqi Freedom, Doug is a young, single guy, and this is his last tour in the army.

Doc—Staff Sergeant A. Lott is the team medic and normally the senior medic on the ground in most scenarios. Eventually awarded the coveted Army Commendation Medal with Valor for his actions during the final offensive, Doc is the main prankster on the team. His dry, sarcastic humor is rivaled only by Goose. Doc is a veteran of multiple tours in Operation Iraqi Freedom.

Cowboy—Sergeant First Class John Johnson is a veteran of numerous tours in Iraq and brings a wealth of knowledge and experience to the team. He gets his nickname from his preferences of roping, rodeo, driving big trucks, and living on a ranch. He is the "make it happen" guy on the team, working everything from training Iraqis on maintenance, communications, and weapons to taking care of team vehicles and communications equipment.

Cowboy is a veteran of so many wars that I have lost track of them all.

Sanchez—Captain Dee Sanchez is the assistant operations officer and works with training Iraqis and preparing operations orders. A native of the lovely island of Puerto Rico, he is divorced and likes fast cars (don't we all?). His *is* extremely fast. He is a suave guy, and he works with Captain Zabilinski in operations.

Bolt—Captain Chris Bolt is the other logistics guy on the team. His primary duties are as the human resources officer and headquarters company advisor. Bolt is married with kids and can't wait to get home to them. He is a veteran of Operation Iraqi Freedom.

G (not the original)—Sergeant First Class Brian Gerschank he is the communications trainer and team communications guy. He is a black man trapped in a white body, as he likes to say. Brian is from the Bronx in New York and is a gigantic man at 5 feet, 2 inches. We originally deployed without him, and he met up with us in Iraq after a few months.

Tootsie Roll Bank—Sergeant Tom Loudhorn is the team logistics noncommissioned officer and my assistant. His naming is better left to the imagination. He is a really big guy and very intimidating to an average-sized Iraqi. Sometimes when the Iraqi police would get out of line during training, we would send him over to scare them a little. He is a veteran of Operation Iraqi Freedom.

Geeb—Captain Mattias Black is the Intelligence Officer (S2) and trainer for the team. Geeb is a combined nickname of Naqeeb (meaning captain in Arabic) and Goober, given to him by an Iraqi general and Master Sergeant Calderon, due to his alleged involvement in a potential international incident. Geeb is an ex-tanker and a stocky guy, and he had a tour in Operation Iraqi Freedom during 2004.

Goose—Captain G.—yours truly. Apparently, I resemble the character nicknamed Goose (Tom Cruz's character's buddy) in the movie *Top Gun*. I am the executive officer to Major Strongarm and the primary logistics trainer. I am a veteran of Desert Storm and Operation Iraqi Freedom 2003 to 2004.

Colonel Rasmun (Iraqi) Rasmun is the Iraqi Battalion commander of the Iraqi unit that we are advising (he is our third in a period of two months, but he stays with us the rest of our tour in Iraq). He speaks excellent English and is adept and experienced in dealing with Americans (most Iraqis aren't). He was a general in the Iraqi Army and fought in Desert Shield and Desert Storm (against us).

General Muhammed (Iraqi)—The Iraqi Brigade commander over the Iraqi unit that we advise. He does not speak English. He is probably somewhat sympathetic to Jeesh al-Mahdi (to be explained later).

Colonel Ate (Iraqi)—The second Iraqi Battalion commander of the Iraqi unit that we are advising. He was the first commander we worked with in our Iraqi unit, And he was eventually fired and was in league with Jeesh al-Mahdi (which was not uncommon for this unit when we arrived).

Lieutenant Allah—He is an Iraqi platoon leader and is moved to several jobs throughout the year. He saves our interpreter and is the platoon leader in charge during what is known as "The

Firefight." He is an extremely dedicated Iraqi officer, and the guys on our team had great respect for him. He is also a bit of a jokester at times.

Prologue

> "Hope is a state of mind, not of the world. Hope, in this deep and powerful sense, is not the same as joy that things are going well, or willingness to invest in enterprises that are obviously heading for success, but rather an ability to work for something because it is good." —Va'clav Havel

Hope is a wonderful feeling that soldiers in a war do not have the luxury to feel. Commanders, leaders, and soldiers do not count on hope to get them through the day. They plan, inspect, practice, and apply methods in such a manner to rule out any need for hope. This creates a confidence that is the essence of the United States Army.

President George W. Bush decided in 2006 to change the course of the war in Iraq. He moved key generals to different positions and invested heavily in counterinsurgency doctrine (COIN, in military terms). Not since the Vietnam conflict has an insurgency taken hold like the one that began in Iraq in approximately April 2004.

The new course required the extensive use of military forces in a large "surge" of tens of thousands of additional service members in Iraq. The new strategy also required a surge of military advisors to train and equip the defunct Iraqi Armed Forces. The thought process behind the surge of advisors was that once the Iraqi military took over the job of security in Iraq, the U.S. forces could come home. This new strategy requires an extensive use of military advisors (U.S. soldiers embedded in the Iraqi military) to assist and advise Iraqi units. Military advisors belong to teams called Military Transition Teams (MTTs). MTTs have the difficult task of advising and training a foreign military and handing over the security of a nation.

Advisors are war fighters, peacekeepers, trainers, and everything else in between. This story is about our transition team's experiences in Iraq in 2007 and 2008, following this historic change in the course of the Iraq war. Our experiences as a team are unique and are representative of this time in history. Perhaps they can bring to light some of the unique difficulties faced by Iraqi and U.S. soldiers and civilians who lived and fought at this time. This book started as a military journal. It has become a work written for military personnel, their family members, and those who are interested in knowing what is really going on with transition teams in Iraq. These stories reflect extensively on the discord of existence in Iraq.

I found it ironic that our team's first assignment location was a forward combat outpost named Hope, and so I chose to include it in the book's title. The commentary, background, and stories hopefully will provide a reference and an entertaining account of our team's experiences in difficult situations. The book focuses mainly on the MTT Blacksheep team's experiences in Baghdad, Iraq.

The book begins with a sobering experience, upon our initial arrival to Iraq—sobering because most of the team members were mentally unprepared for the experiences of daily combat in Iraq. A few knew what we were getting into, but overall the majority of us had no idea. The book reflects back to the formation of our team and our training experiences. It follows our yearlong tour as we mentally and physically learned to cope with extreme situations. The stories do not always follow a chronological order, but the sequence is evident as you read along the chapters. Ultimately, we all survived and made it home to the ones we love.

My friend James and I were talking about this book and how and why it was to be written. We realized that we were exposed to things on a daily basis that are so difficult to imagine that you have no basis to compare them with anything else in your life. The experiences take on an almost dreamlike feeling, and because of this we would find ourselves constantly questioning if what we were witnessing was really happening.

Since my tour in Iraq, I have spoken with numerous other friends and colleagues who have experienced this same feeling. The book's chapters are thus written in such a way as to bring these feelings out almost in the same order as they occurred.

We continued our discussion, and my friend said for me to not be too wrapped up in understanding why the things were happening but instead to just write them down. It was my task, he told me, to finish the job (my deployment), return home, and live a normal life again. Most of the experiences our team had in a given month in Iraq were things that the average American will not see in his or her entire lifetime. I felt at the time that our deployment was more than a bad experience: It was a story unfolding, and I was the witness to this story. Throughout my deployment, I noticed that I would see something crazy and say the words "holy shit," and that it was usually a significant event worthy of writing down in my notebook. Writing a book in the middle of a chaotic and dangerous deployment can be an overwhelming task, but I knew from the start that it had to be done.

I sometimes compare the experiences to the dreamlike feeling that comes when one wakes from a nightmare. That moment comes when the nightmare ends and the awareness of the dreamlike instance is with you. You are not quite awake, but you're not quite asleep, either.

Keep in mind as you read this book that most of the characters in these situations were under a great deal of stress. The craziness of these situations was usually elevated by heightened emotions, adrenaline, energy drinks, a day or two without sleep, the smell of burnt gunpowder and burning trash, rockets exploding, gunfire cracking, eighty pounds of equipment on your body, and dehydration from temperatures often more than one hundred twenty degrees Fahrenheit.

The sensation of things seeming to slow down during extremely dangerous combat situations happened frequently to us. That sensation stems from a jolt of an excessive amount of adrenaline and then the subsequent total focus resulting from the sudden abundance of that natural chemical in the bloodstream. As you read each chapter, recall this slowing down or dreamlike feeling that we experienced during those harrowing situations.

The reader should also keep in mind that a soldier on a combat outpost has very little access to stress-relieving outlets. It feels like being in a prison. Soldiers feel "confined" most of the time, and then when they do get to leave the compound, it is to go on a dangerous combat mission. Soldiers look for outlets to help them to cope with it. Mine was typing and drafting notes for the book. Most mornings I would wake up at 4:00 or 5:00 am and just begin typing. Writing this book became an outlet that allowed me to cope with the bad dreams and experiences from the previous day.

Iraq is a confusing place for a soldier. We are taught (and taught well) the craft of wielding our nation's mighty arsenal and bringing it to bear on our enemies in an intense manner. Then we are asked to pick our enemy up and embrace them … to provide hope. This situation creates a duality of feelings in most soldiers as they go about their day-to-day activities in Iraq. Mixed with positive and negative emotions, you search your feelings, looking for a better sense of purpose to justify why your friends are dying. What am I fighting for? What are my friends dying for? These are the questions on a soldier's mind in a protracted war. When it is all said and done, it is for the people on your team that you are fighting for. It is for them that you die. It is for them that the path becomes justified and meaningful. None of the other reasons really matter when the first bullets fly.

My friend continued with his advice to me. He said that when I got home, I should take my photos, videos, uniforms, journals, and equipment and pack them in a box, and then put them away in a closet. Go on with your life from that point where you left off before the war, he told me, and maybe on some faraway day, when all the nightmares are long forgotten and you are an old man, you can pull these things out and dust them off. That would be a good time to pull out a book about your experiences. This is that book—and these are the dreams … of hope.

My thanks go out to God, my family, my contributors, my editors, and my friends. I don't know if my team was expecting quite a work of this type, but for all it is worth, I hope that you guys enjoy it. *Blacksheep*! §

1

First Month in Iraq

"Toto, I've a feeling we're not in Kansas anymore..."

"It is not the ones you hear that kill you; it's the ones you don't hear ... that kill you."—team member's quote, in answer to my constant question about mortar rounds

OUR FIRST MONTH IN IRAQ—HANDOVER BETWEEN OLD TEAM AND OUR CURRENT TEAM IN PROGRESS

The team had been physically in Iraq for only a couple of weeks. It was over 115 degrees Fahrenheit by 10:00 am on most days. It smelled like burning trash everywhere. The fine, Arabian dust in the air filled our noses up so much that we had to wash them out with water every couple of hours so that we could breathe. Driving along the roads and routes in Iraq, we saw nothing but trash, raw sewage in the streets, traffic, and more trash. We were in the middle of replacing a transition team headed up by marines. Several dangerous combat vehicle patrols in Sadr City had focused us into a careful application of the tactics we recently learned during our training at Fort Riley, Kansas. At the time, I was unprepared for the constant stress involved with daily trips "outside the wire." Outside the wire is the common phrase used by soldiers to describe a mission outside of a protected area, into a dangerous combat zone. We were on our third or fourth patrol, and my eyes were sore from the intense, focused staring involved with visually searching for improvised explosive devices (IEDs), explosively formed penetrators (EFPs), and snipers along the trash covered roadsides. In training, they tell you that insurgents hide explosive devices in trash and trash piles. What they don't tell you is that the entire country of Iraq is *covered* with trash.

This visual searching is split among different team members in the vehicle who watch different portions of the road, looking for explosive devices. As if things weren't bad enough, it doesn't help to hear the "ca-clink" and feel the gunner's feet hit you as he chambers a large round and spins the gun turret around in the up-armored Humvee to identify his next target. The M240B machine gun is an automatic weapon about three feet from your right ear when you are driving the Humvee. Any "action" that happens results in a deafening blast from the weapon, as the gunner fires it and empties about a pound of hot brass that rains down on you. Commands are screamed or given via radio within the vehicles and among the various other vehicles in the convoy, so there is a constant awareness of the overall situation among all personnel. Like a large, single entity or a lone, collective brain, we all simultaneously understand what is going on. Fifteen months later, after I returned from Iraq, I was still unable to stop my eyes from scanning the road in my neighborhood as I went to the store for groceries or whatever—and I still look for snipers on bridges.

On this particular day, we were headed on a patrol. After a briefing on the previous day's explosions—mortar rounds, explosive devices, and other attacks in the area—I remember quietly praying to myself and thanking whoever designed the program. It overwhelmingly focused on maneuvering, communicating, and firing techniques. An army cadence was rattling in my brain as I had this thought sitting in the Humvee … how did it go? I sang it out, "Shoot, move, and communicate … boom."

Boom! A large explosion rocked the armored Humvee we were sitting in outside the Joint Security Station. The Security Station had been the target of numerous mortar attacks in recent weeks, leading up to this incident. Minutes before, the team's noncommissioned officer in charge had been arguing with one of the team members about staying inside the vehicles. It was counter to what most soldiers were taught to do. In years gone by, you would "dismount" and exit your vehicle when parked. Then you would "pull security" around the vehicle. Those days were gone. The procedure now was to remain in the vehicles (due to the armor) and to be prepared to immediately exit the area. Later, we adopted a different strategy that seemed to make more sense to me—drop off the folks that need to go in and get the hell out of there.

In Desert Storm, I was once in a convoy close enough to the battle to have my vehicle rocked by an explosion. This explosion at the security station was much closer and was followed by the now familiar sound of small, metal shrapnel raining down against the Humvee's armor, which sounds like a hard rain or hail hitting the top of some aluminum siding. The difference is, if this rain hits you … you will die.

An experienced, noncommissioned officer (NCO) in my vehicle, with four tours (more than four years of combat) in Iraq under his belt, said, "That was close." We had heard numerous rounds land and other explosions in the last couple of weeks, including one small mortar attack on the forward operating base where we lived. These rounds were directed at us.

"What do we do?" I asked excitedly, but trying to maintain an air of confidence in my voice, as I was the senior person in the vehicle at the time.

"Nothing" was the answer I got. "If the rounds are this close and you try to move the vehicles, you could run into them. Wait until the next one comes in, and pay attention to the direction it's fired from." This guy was an artillery NCO (now called an effects NCO) with seventeen years in the army, and he knew what he was talking about. We called him Cowboy, because he raised horses and lived in Texas.

The next set of rounds was closer, and the impact from it hit the rear of one of our vehicles. "Move the vehicle forward, Captain," Cowboy said, in a loud, directive tone. As a driver for the lead vehicle, I had become accustomed to taking direction from the gunner. Several of the vehicles had sustained damage from that blast, but thankfully we were all buttoned up (securely sitting inside) in one of the vehicles, and no one had been hurt. I was scared, but not so scared that I could not function.

I moved the vehicle forward, and it felt as if things were happening in slow motion. My adrenaline was flowing, and my heart was pumping so hard I felt I could almost hear it beating. The other vehicles, many with flat tires and other damage, followed us. We positioned the vehicles against the eastern perimeter wall of HESCO barriers (large, eight-foot-tall wire baskets with a liner filled with dirt), making it extremely difficult for someone to shoot at us and drop a mortar accurately and directly onto us.

The strategy worked well and is a testament to the fact that experienced noncommissioned officers are worth their weight in gold. I had no problems taking direction from this guy. He was not very talkative, but his experience could not be equaled.

I quietly thought to myself, *Why did I join the army?* I often did this when in a situation like this, when I was picturing so many other places that I would rather be.

During the random explosions of mortars, artillery, small arms fire, and other explosions I had encountered to date, I had asked one question many times: "How do you know the difference between outgoing and incoming rounds and explosions, and how do you know when it is coming toward you?" I was worried because, to me, no one seemed to be responding appropriately to the sounds (i.e., heading for a cement bunker nearby).

I always got the same answer: "Don't worry; it's the ones you don't hear that kill you." This was the answer I got from Cowboy, and he was right. We were still in the same spot, and now the incoming mortars that hit us exploded and rocked the vehicles right as they impacted. The other sounds of mortars I heard were whistling sounds, and you could almost tell the direction they were traveling if you listened closely. You could almost begin to make out whether they were large or small mortars. It takes time and experience to train yourself to do something like that automatically. Just like the eyes looking for snipers, it is something your ears will never stop listening for.

During our training at Fort Riley, we were required to do a tire changing drill on a Humvee. At that time, we had thought that the whole thing was stupid and a waste of time. Now, in combat, we were next to the barriers with a bunch of blown-out tires—looking for jacks, lug nuts, boards to prop things up, and so on. Luckily for us, a maintenance team was close by and responded with an additional tire (we needed five) to get us operational and back on the road.

I did not know it at the time, but a few of us had just earned the Combat Action Badge (CAB) within the first two weeks of hitting the ground (arriving) in Iraq. The badge is similar to the Combat Infantryman's Badge that is given to infantrymen in combat, but the CAB is for noninfantry personnel. Being fired on by mortar rounds apparently was good enough to get the badge. Later, we would all earn the badge again … in fact, *many* times over.

At the time, I was thinking, *This is bad.* Things were going to get worse before they got any better. How could anyone survive a year of this? Over the course of the next year, we would use every task that we had been taught in our training at Fort Riley. Over and over … and over again. Our little team was one of the better teams that went through the training at Fort Riley at the time. Overall, we had drawn a decent lot of people assigned to our team—and we could all shoot all of the weapons really well.

Originally, we were told we would be headed out to western Iraq, in the Fallujah area, but were changed at the last minute while in Kuwait, waiting to come to Iraq. This was a great disservice to us and allowed for no prior planning on the specifics of our area. Differences in religion, government, tactical forces, enemy, and so on were things to be taken into consideration when training for a specific area.

We were as proactive with training and planning as we could be while at Fort Riley. We used our spare time to prepare well, but the one thing we could not get ready for was the heat. The heat on that day in Iraq was around 119 degrees Fahrenheit when standing in the sun outside in Sadr City. It was a far different place from the cold Kansas plains that we had just left a few weeks prior. §

2

Left Out in the Cold

Let no man's soul cry out "If only I had the proper training." —World War II poster

TWO MONTHS PRIOR TO OUR DEPARTURE TO IRAQ—WE ARE AT THE BEGINNING OF THE MILITARY ADVISOR TRAINING PROGRAM AT FORT RILEY, KANSAS

On our convoy back after changing the damaged tires, I thought about our training at Fort Riley. The extreme heat of this day made my mind flash back to another incident of extreme temperature, one while we were in training in Kansas. The temperature outside was then a bitter negative eight degrees Fahrenheit on a pitch black and snowy evening, about a month into our training. We were ten miles away from anything in any direction, at a weapons firing range on the flat plains of an army post called Fort Riley, Kansas. It was cold and windy, with an inch or two of snow already on the ground. It had been snowing lightly all evening, but the snow was now coming down more heavily. Who knows what the wind chill factor was, with all that wind? We estimated it to be about negative twenty degrees. There was a tower overlooking the range, where the operations personnel screamed out commands that we could barely make out with the wind howling and our earplugs in our ears (a safety precaution due to the weapons fire). The place had a bathroom facility and a small building with heat that we were huddled in. Our team chief and others were slightly frostbitten and just plain *cold*. We were at the end of an extremely long day of training, huddled in a building that had just enough warmth inside to allow you to get some slightly warm coffee and to stave off the bitter chill of the winter night's air.

In any other unit, these conditions would probably cause the training to be called off for that day. Not in this unit. We were aligning our sites and qualifying our weapons by shooting rounds at pop-up silhouette targets out to the 50-meter, 100-meter, 200-meter, and 300-meter targets. This is a difficult task during the day … and an even more difficult task using our night vision and lasers at night (nobody hit the 300-meter target on this night). Yes, we were lying in the snow, in the bitter cold, trying to determine a target with no light to see. Normally, the moon would be out and would light things up a bit for you to see a target. Not tonight.

It was a difficult task for those of us who had never used the equipment before. The technology was all fairly new and definitely had some tricks to it. All of the guys on our team could shoot well, but this new equipment and the cold weather were challenging. The range cadre had been outside the entire time of the training (four to five hours), and they were also freezing their butts off. After we were done qualifying and hitting several of the targets in these conditions, we could go inside the building and warm up.

They began to try and speed things up by providing individual coaching to each of the firers on the line.

Most of us got it on the first or second try. A few of us didn't. Sanchez was having a hard time qualifying and he was told he had to go out for a third time. His glasses were fogging up, he couldn't get the night goggles or the laser to work right, and he couldn't hit the targets. What he really needed was some coaching. Everybody was too frozen to go back out again. The instructors running the range were busy, but they were completely frozen and barely coherent. No one was paying enough attention to realize the help this guy needed. I could not stand to see him left out in the cold again with no one to coach him. I put my gear on, grabbed my Kevlar helmet, and walked out the door behind him into the bitter, cold night. We adjusted the weapon and talked through the targets, and he got it, this time on the first try! It was ironic, because no one should have been left alone in the cold doing a task like that. The army doesn't work that way. Not my army anyway.

We might as well have moved out to the heavy weapons range with sleeping bags and lived there for the entire course. We spent a great deal of time at that range. At the time we hated it, but when we got to Iraq and realized how much those skills were needed, we were really glad to have them. The range was loud … *really* loud … and really cold. A crew-served weapon is a large, automatic weapon that requires a crew of a couple of personnel to operate and assist with firing the weapon, because it is large and the ammunition is heavy and linked together. Compared with my job in support units, I would have been lucky to have actually qualified once a year with my assigned 9-millimeter pistol. I fired more ammunition in that ninety days at this course than I had fired in my entire eighteen years in the military—no exaggerations!

I had never seen such a cold place in my life. While I was driving to Fort Riley, the windshield wiper fluid inside of the pump and wiper lines froze solid. The stuff was rated to negative 10 degrees Fahrenheit. It was amazing! I had the heat on in the car with a full complement of clothing on, and I was still freezing. I stopped at a store that had stacks and stacks of boxes of wiper fluid and antifreeze all over. It should have clicked in my head why they were there (the antifreeze goes in your wiper fluid), but it didn't. This was a bad sign, knowing that we had months of outdoor training ahead. When we had arrived for our training at Fort Riley, the temperature was negative 8 degrees, and when we had finished and traveled to Kuwait, the temperature there hit 125 degrees, a difference of 133 degrees!

My buddy in the training class ahead of mine told me to bring a car. The post was massive in size, and yet the teams were told prior to coming to Fort Riley that they did not need cars. Because there were no regular buses, I don't know what they were trying to do with us, but you damn sure needed your car. These were our last days of freedom before going away on a yearlong deployment of living with Iraqis in a foreign land. We wanted to get out as much as possible and taste civilian life while we could. A plate of fajitas and a beer at Chili's never tasted as good as it did after six straight days of twelve to fourteen hours of constant training per day.

We were living in barracks on top of each other like privates in basic training. This is not typical for a group of senior personnel who mostly were majors, captains, master sergeants, and sergeants first class. It got old, fast. The facilities were in good condition. but it is still barracks life: bunk beds, communal showers, no Internet, a ten-minute walk to get to your car. Limited food selections were available in the chow hall. We were a bunch of senior leaders who normally would be separated from this and put in our own room away from the soldiers. The problem was that this time, we were all senior leaders and there were no soldiers. We had to do everything ourselves.

Overall, the training was exactly what the command sergeant major (CSM) of the brigade tasked to train us described it as: it was a "leveling" course. Some team members were more experienced in combat tasks and infantry tactics, but the large majority were not, and it was difficult for the infantry guys to understand how we support guys were not adept in infantry tactics. It was equally as hard for us as supply and logistics guys to understand how bad the infantry guys were at planning and supporting operations.

The army took a brigade at Fort Riley and designated them the trainers of the transition teams. I wasn't able to find out how the unit was chosen or why; normally this type of mission is not given to a standard Army unit. Training and Doctrine Command is the organization normally responsible for training for all soldiers. These soldiers training us were combat veterans, and a few of them had some experience dealing with Iraqis. Overall, the units training the transition teams had little or no practical experience with transition teams. This stuff was too new for them. There were civilian contractors hired to assist in some of the more technical areas, such as language training. However, the language training was too sparsely distributed throughout the course for us to grasp it. Learning Arabic in a couple of hour-long sessions over a ninety-day period doesn't work for most people. Additionally, we were not chosen for this assignment due to our ability to grasp the Arabic language (an extremely difficult language to learn, in my opinion).

Over the course of three months, we received training and instruction in a myriad of tasks related to combat and advising in Iraq. The format was similar to the required training that most large brigades in the army are required to undertake prior to an Iraq deployment. But this training was specifically tailored to us. Classes ranged anywhere from explosive device awareness to field hygiene and sanitation. There were also classes on intelligence, staff planning, Iraqi culture, combatives, and others. Suffice it to say that the training program was sufficiently well thought out, given the makeup of our teams.

It was obvious right when we saw the team's composition that life was going to be a challenge over the course of our deployment. Combining a major, several captains, senior NCOs, and a few other folks makes for some interesting discussions about who is in charge of what. These people are all used to being in charge of something … but we were all chiefs and no braves. We started out at Fort Riley missing two NCOs, and these were arguably who we needed the most in logistics and communications. Later on in the deployment, our replacements would arrive and fill our shortages.

While at Fort Riley, we were originally told we were going to Fallujah. The Battle of Fallujah was still fresh in our minds as army leaders, and we envisioned and discussed at length what the situation would be like. When we arrived in Kuwait, we were then switched to Sadr City, and our designation was changed from Military Transition Team (MTT) to National Police Transition Team (NPTT). The staffing of our team was specifically as a MTT, so we were confused about why they would use us as a NPTT. We never got an answer on that. At the time, no one had really taken the time to explain the difference to us, and most of the folks at Fort Riley and the Iraqi Assistance Group in Kuwait didn't know the difference (or didn't care).

Amid the tactical tasks, we trained on Iraqi military logistics, Iraqi military intelligence, Iraqi military personnel issues, and on other issues. Throughout our training, we would ask about the National Police (NP) systems. No one in any of our training or in Iraq had any answers about the NP. We found out later that the polite silence when we asked a question about how the NP system compares with the Iraqi Army simply meant that they were corrupt. It also meant that many, many folks were holding up their hands and saying, "We tried, but it is a hopeless cause, so we are sending you to go fix them."

The previous year, 2006, was the "year of the police," as they had called the U.S.-led hiring campaign in Iraq. What that meant was that pretty much anybody could get into the police. Now the corruption was rampant. Now we had to go deal with them. This we were doing with very little resources and guidance, and with little to no information on the specifics of the NP.

Our team wondered aloud on many occasions how we could be taking on a Special Forces mission (to advise and train foreign forces). A Special Forces soldier spends several years in various technical training schools learning such areas as languages, medical skills, and weapons. We were being sent to live and work and fight with indigenous Iraqi forces who had minimal training and a team of staff guys with a couple months of training. This was going to be *fun* (note the sarcasm).

Each team had two logistics guys. This meant that the majority of my entire advanced course of peers was deployed to Iraq. I had just come from eight months of training at Fort Lee in our captains course. Everyone in my class of ninety or so personnel, except for about four people, were sent on transition teams. People find that hard to believe, but it is the truth. It was timing; they needed the officers, and we were the most easily accessible pool to pull from. Many regular units were going to be without senior captains to command units while we were gone.

The training primarily focused exactly on what it was supposed to, in my opinion: surviving in combat. Shooting all types of weapons, understanding how to move together and coordinate as teams, and communicating via sophisticated communications devices—those were the primary tasks. There were many other tasks in training to deal with the Iraqis, such as language training and contracting, but the focus was not so much on these tasks. Overall, the training did what it was apparently designed to do: train us for serious combat. If you screw up the combat part, you are dead, and no advising will be going on.

Back at Fort Riley, our training was in the cold, and in many ways the cold began to get our attention. The bitter cold of that night training on the weapons firing range in Kansas had foreshadowed the hard reality of our upcoming situation. In the very near future, we would be out on our own, living and working with the Iraqis—

out on our own, doing our mission with very little resources. When left out in the cold to your own devices, you can either freeze to death or you can solve the issues and go back in to the warm room. Throughout our tour in Iraq, we would be left on our own many times to solve things for ourselves. As it turned out, this was only the beginning, a hint of what was ahead for us in the extreme temperatures of Sadr City, Iraq. §

3

The Solution and the Problem

"The only difference between a problem and a solution is that people understand the solution."—Charles F. Kettering

When we arrived in Iraq, we quickly came to realize the importance of Sadr City to what is now called by many Iraqis as Iraq's civil war. Sadr City (formerly known as Saddam City) was Saddam Hussein's solution to the sectarian issues behind the civil war in Iraq. This is important to understand, as it defines the majority of problems we dealt with in Sadr City and specifically with the National Police (NP) during our tour. Over the course of our tour, we would eventually work with both the NP and the Iraqi Army, but nine or ten months of our tour was spent mainly with the NP.

A few guys on our team had been exposed to the intricacies of Iraqi cultural and political issues prior to our arrival, but the majority of us had not. The main issues in Iraqi culture revolve around fundamental differences of Islamic interpretation, and the problems go back thousands of years.

Sadr City is, and has been since before April 2004, the primary haven of the Jeesh al-Mahdi (JAM). Literally interpreted, it means the Army of the Mahdi. Since the majority of Al-Qaeda members in Iraq were driven out or captured, the Jeesh al-Mahdi has risen to become a threat. The Shia Muslims (more specifically, Jeesh al-Mahdi–sponsored Shia) are heavily involved in politics and have gained control over the ministry of the interior. In the course of our yearlong tour in Iraq, we would witness an amazing change of thought or approach to dealing with Jeesh al-Mahdi. When we first arrived in Iraq, Jeesh al-Mahdi was the enemy, but things change constantly in Iraq. A month or so before we left Iraq, Jeesh al-Mahdi was now viewed as a legitimate Iraqi organization.

What does that mean on the ground in Sadr City, when you are being shot at by a group of Shia guys, wearing all-black outfits, on a 110-degree day, with a rocket-propelled grenade and some AK-47 automatic rifles? Not much—we shoot back, get in a little scuffle, maybe capture some guys and equipment. Then we wake up the next day and do it again. To the Iraqis, the Jeesh al-Mahdi represents much more. Black-clad males driving BMWs and Mercedes represent power and authority in Sadr City. This is a very important concept in Iraqi culture and is similar to the perception of the Italian Mafia in many ways.

The Shia are viewed by the Sunni Muslims as being a little too extreme. Speaking to some of the older Iraqis, I was told that in years gone by, the Shia would come out once a year for long parades or processions through Baghdad. As they walked down the street, they would actually physically cut themselves or flail themselves. This was too much for the Sunni to watch. Saddam Hussein moved all the Shia into their own city so that they could do this and practice their own version of Islam. Other stories I have heard about the Shia are that they enjoy a good uprising or demonstration, and that Saddam Hussein had to quell the violence in Sadr City on more than one occasion by force. After one particular uprising, Saddam Hussein purportedly said these words, as the Sunnis love to tell it: "All will be quiet in Al-Thawra [Sadr City] tonight or I will be watching the sun rise over a peaceful area of land in the morning." What Hussein meant was that if the Shia did not stop demonstrating in Sadr City, he was going to use the military to completely level the city and kill everyone.

Sadr City—once known as Al-Thawra (revolution), then as Saddam City, and most recently named after the father of Iraqi Ayatollah Muqtada al-Sadr—is humongous and covers a large area of Baghdad. It houses several million people and is currently the soda and bottling center of all Iraq.

The city has extensive infrastructure problems. Streets and markets are flooded with raw sewage from years of waste. Trash is dumped in the street and burned at night. Imagine a scene from the John Carpenter film *Escape from New York*, where lead character Snake Pliskin is searching the futuristic prison city: barricades in the streets, fires, sewage, trash piles ... that is Sadr City.

The Mahdi is the twelfth Imam in the Shia religion. They believe the Imam will return, and Muqtada al-Sadr uses this belief in telling Iraqis that the Americans have come to Iraq to kill the Mahdi. The Grand Ayatollah Muhammad al-Sadr was Muqtada al-Sadr's father, who was assassinated by Saddam Hussein in the city Al-Najaf in central Iraq in 1999. His son formed the Jama'at al-Sadr al-Thani (Association of the Second al-Sadr) as the key organization of the al-Sadr family network. Muqtada al-Sadr is in league with Iran, but many believe that he is tired of the association.

The Army of the Mahdi

The Mahdi Army was formed after the fall of Saddam in 2003. The United States actually had a hand in making al-Sadr into such a celebrity because they held talks with him. In 2004, the Jeesh al-Mahdi was estimated to consist of about five hundred to a thousand trained combatants with another five to six thousand active participants. The militia has participated in assassinations of rival clerics and has disrupted the security of Baghdad on numerous occasions since 2004. The militia has attempted to gain control of various government and police buildings using organized attacks with small arms fire and rocket-propelled grenades.

From 2004 to 2007 the Jeesh al-Mahdi was involved in numerous battles and altercations throughout Baghdad. Sadr City, Baghdad, and Basrah are the main areas used by Jeesh al-Mahdi. Sadr City is mostly Shiite territory, and Prime Minister Nuri al-Maliki blocked coalition attempts to police Sadr City because it was a main source of his political strength. By the start of 2007, al-Maliki discontinued this support, and more than six hundred members of the Jeesh al-Mahdi were arrested in Sadr City. In February 2007, U.S. forces were granted operational flexibility and they moved into Sadr City. They arrested Deputy Health Minister Hakim al-Zamili for funneling money to the Jeesh al-Mahdi. Muqtada al-Sadr told his forces not to take up arms and to stop operations, and he then fled to Iran.

A recent cease-fire with the Jeesh al-Mahdi has kept things quiet for several months. The sheiks from Sadr City attended a conference for a possible peace accord. The infighting of elements of the Jeesh Al-Mahdi, the special groups of the Jeesh Al-Mahdi, and its rival group Badr Corporation (another Jeesh Al-Mahdi organization), has risen over the course of 2007. This has resulted in numerous clashes in the Sadr City and New Baghdad area. Meanwhile, in 2007, the NP is the Iraqi government organization providing security in the Sadr City and New Baghdad area, and we are the military advisors to them.§

4

Year of the Police

"'Year of the Police' a rocky one so far in Iraq"—
Stars and Stripes headline, March 2006

THE SITUATION WITH THE IRAQI NATIONAL POLICE WHEN WE ARRIVED

The situation with the Iraqi NP was more than a little rocky when we arrived. A little background is necessary prior to discussing our team's adventures. A few Department of Defense (DOD) press releases provide background about the situation with the NP prior to our arrival. The Iraqi NP are a military force (like an army unit) responsible for most of the area where we were stationed during our tour. During the time of the first Iraqi national election in January 2005, the parliament and the ministries of Iraq split along sectarian lines. The NP report to the Ministry of the Interior, and the Iraqi Army reports to the Ministry of Defense. The National Police operate in a similar manner to the Iraqi Army but with far less resources. The Eighth Brigade of the Second Division was our higher headquarters, and a few years ago it was an Iraqi Army unit. It is unknown why the unit became a National Police brigade.

We saw great progress in the Iraqis over the course of a yearlong tour. In the months before we redeployed, the National Police commanders were taking orders from the Iraqi Army general in the area and doing well. In addition, the Iraq Army and NP commanders were meeting regularly about security issues in the area.

The most recent references regarding the NP in existence at the time were the following articles. They demonstrate the difficulties with corruption that existed prior to our arrival. The reorganizations and removals of commanders and movements of units referred to in the excerpts occurred just a few months before we arrived. Serious efforts at training, equipping, and supplying the unit were not yet under way. These efforts would eventually fall to us to complete, even though three years of transition teams had already been through Iraq and worked with the unit. The security situation had been so bad in the past that the American advisors could not realistically be stationed with the National Police and still perform their mission. Again, they were looking at us to do this. In army terminology, we were to be at the tip of the spear on this initiative. This meant that we were the ones who where actually out making the most difference in the war. As the article below indicates, most of the brigade and battalion leadership had been swapped out prior to our arrival. This was a good thing. The article continues on to indicate how and why the units were trained and moved to certain locations.

(Note—The following quotes are General Peterson's answers to reporters at a DOD press briefing on 6 October 2006.)

"The Eighth Brigade and its units were inspected in early August. There are three battalions in the brigade, and two of the battalions barely passed the inspection. In addition to that, we had some difficulty with the performance of that brigade on their specific missions within the Baghdad Security Plan."

"The brigade commander had been relieved of his responsibilities, and then you add to that the issues that we had with the Second Battalion Commander—who, by the way, has been arrested for possible complicity."

"The minister felt that the rest of the forces of the battalions and brigades … were at risk … he pulled them all together, put them in their own garrison locations, and they will begin an intensive reorganization process …"

"Well, the Second Battalion of the Eighth Brigade has been implicated on a raid of a meat processing factory wherein 22 individuals—it was a little over 20 individuals were kidnapped, and later, seven of them were found killed. Again, the commander, because the unit and the organization was [sic] identified as potentially being responsible for committing this transgression, has been arrested. And the organization is currently under investigation."

"What we know is the majority of people that were working in the plant were Sunni, and so potentially this could be a sectarian issue."

"I think the [date of the raid] was about a week ago now. I'm uncertain as to the exact date."

"The national police organizations basically were formed and were primarily focused really on military tasks. And for the past two years plus, they've been performing more military like tasks—raids, cordon searches, those kinds of things. They went through about six weeks of training. They had about 15 hours to 20 hours of rule of law, protection of human rights training. But it was mixed on the amount of police training that they received."

"The national police force of Iraq is a paramilitary organization. It is an organization that is intended to bridge—to provide a bridge between the police forces themselves and the Iraqi Army. …"

The following paragraphs are from my own notes about the situation with the NP.

The training referred to in the briefing is held at Numaniyah Academy and was a process referred to as "re-blueing," meaning that they were being retrained to be better police than they were before. Almost every transition team that we ran into told us their unit had been through this training facility. After being retrained, the policemen are given a new, very distinguishable blue uniform, similar to the U.S. Army uniform. The new blue uniform notified the population that the policemen had been retrained. The perception of the public and the army about the National Police was that they were corrupt and using their position to accomplish murder, kidnapping, and other serious acts of sectarian violence throughout Iraq (which they *were* doing, according to the above-quoted articles). This perception changed dramatically in our unit when we left Iraq.

The National Police proved themselves to us and to the local area who counted on them to keep the neighborhoods (*mulhallas*) secure. Our Iraqi unit eventually began to provide us with good information on a daily basis and was operating the unit in an effective manner when we left them.

After they were retrained at Numaniyah, the police were then restationed at Combat Outpost Hope. It was a good idea, but all we got to see were the aftereffects of bad planning and a lack of coordination of these many initiatives. The battalion was a mess when we got them (including no equipment, no supplies, corrupt commanders). There was really no plan to assist or do anything with the battalion after they were re-blued. The press briefing from General Peterson continued on to specifically address training, and his comments are listed below.

On training:

"The phases of the transformation training started off in August with a battalion inspection, and that was focused on accountability of personnel, … equipment … We also did a leader assessment … this led to one of the battalion commanders being replaced and one of the brigade commanders being relieved."

"The second phase is what I just talked to you about, the three weeks of training at Numaniyah. Now, that will be followed by additional training as part of our phase three, where we will then go back and establish a national police training center of excellence …"

The importance of the transition teams to this training academy and to implementing the plan should now be apparent. The transition teams were the glue that made all these initiatives stick. We would guide the Iraqi commanders and assist in developing the units. The point is further driven home by General Pittard, who was the Iraqi Assistance Group (IAG) commander at the time of our arrival.

(Note—the following comments are the words of General Pittard just prior to our arrival in Iraq.)

"If you look at all the transition teams throughout Iraq, it's well above 3,000 coalition soldiers, marines, airmen and Air Force personnel that are involved with that."

"The training model there at Fort Riley … is a 60 day model that truly trains these teams to become advisors. … The first teams to go through Fort Riley went through June 1. Our first teams that have arrived in Iraq after going through that training cycle just arrived two weeks ago. And what a difference they're making."

General Pittard's interview points out the amount of faith put into advisory teams as the solution. The three thousand that he quotes actually became much larger, as the various classes graduated after ours. We were part of one class that comprised more than seven hundred personnel.

Maybe disbanding the Iraqi Army after the initial invasion wasn't such a good idea? The training, reorganization, and other efforts of our military to handle the additional burden to provide "combat advisors" is an intensive effort. Don't forget that our military is also providing combat forces to Iraq on a regular schedule every year.

The year 2006 was called the "Year of the Police." We joked that 2007 would become the year of fixing the police. The retraining efforts, the influx of transition teams, and the heavy recruiting efforts of Iraq Army and National Police recruits were gigantic efforts to get a handle on the issues of the Iraqi armed forces.

Efforts were ongoing with transition teams prior to 2006, but it was the end of 2006 when we started taking counterinsurgency in Iraq seriously. After the training at Fort Riley, teams were sent to training in Kuwait and then on to the Phoenix Academy in Iraq. It was when we arrived at the Phoenix Academy in Iraq that our adventures began. §

5

The Merry-Go-Round

"In Iraq, everything is possible and everything is impossible."—old Iraqi saying

The Phoenix Academy is a little campus in the middle of Iraq where they teach the main principles of counterinsurgency to all incoming transition teams. At the Phoenix Academy, they attempt to link you up with the team that you are replacing. The team we were replacing happened to be teaching one of the classes to us on the relationship of the team with the Iraqi battalion commander. They brought in the person that would soon be our Iraqi battalion commander to introduce himself and to talk to us about what it would be like to work with him and his staff. The outgoing team chief told us that the battalion commander was possibly a supporter of Jeesh al-Mahdi, but we were being sandblasted with so much information it didn't sink in. It was hard for us to decipher the smoke that was being blown our way from the outgoing team. The old team was just giving us the rosy picture of the great things they had done working with the Iraqis and skipping over the bad stuff. Later, we learned that they had really only interacted with the unit on a few occasions in the last couple of months. The security situation was too bad to allow them to live and work with the unit on a regular basis (but we ended up doing just that).

The whole situation struck me as funny because we were being briefed by an Iraqi battalion commander about his expectations of us (it is not an unusual event for an American battalion commander to brief his staff). However, this guy was possibly sympathetic to Jeesh al-Mahdi, and he was telling me what he expected of me. This would be my first experience in navigating the delicate world that a National Police Transition Team (NPTT) lives in on a daily basis.

My inexperience in this area did not prevent my leadership radar from going off about the whole thing. I was feeling like I had just been sold waterfront property in Arizona. Call it your gut feeling or whatever. I have joked with Master Sergeant Calderon on occasion about how long it takes to get this ability. We are both similar in age and years in service. My prior enlisted experience and years as a senior noncommissioned officer had helped develop this ability that most senior leaders in the army possess. You get to that point when things just don't feel right. You can't always immediately identify the cause, but you know when a situation will develop into something bad if you continue down a certain course. I'd had that feeling more times so far in this deployment than the entire time I had been in the army. With NP teams, you deal with uncertain situations on a daily basis.

Now my radar was going off as to why this guy was allowed to come to the Phoenix Academy as a model of what should look right to brief incoming teams. This was our first lesson, and it was not a PowerPoint slide briefing. You had to read between the lines to get the point of this lesson, that very little in Iraq was going to happen the way you were told it would. Use your own judgment, and listen to your gut feeling. These people knew very little about the world they were sending us into to risk our lives and possibly die for. I thought to myself, "is this real … is this truly the way of things?" The dreamy feeling was upon us. Maybe it was the subconscious mind taking the lead from the conscious mind. Hard realities like these are difficult for the conscious mind to accept.

This and many other things would not go as they were supposed to. Many of the briefings at Fort Riley and the Phoenix Academy focused heavily on the Iraqi Army. The instructors had little or no experience and nothing to tell us about the NP. We would stop them and ask them to explain to us the system for the National Police. Because we were assigned as National Police Advisors, we thought it was important to get the specifics. Talking to the instructors was like talking to an eighteen-year-old drive-through clerk at a McDonalds and asking for the obvious things, like napkins and ketchup. The drive-through clerk cops an attitude when you ask for the obvious things you need with your meal, which are sitting in the window where only he can reach them. You can't get them, and he can't seem to fathom that you would possibly need them. That was our experience at the Phoenix Academy.

A few days later, we were at a briefing at the Phoenix Academy from the division level National Police team leader. During the briefing, we saw that his slides showed that our Iraqi battalion commander had been relieved and was a member of the Jeesh al-Mahdi. We were shocked! How could this have been the same guy teaching a class a few days ago in a classroom down the hall? The lesson was clear: nothing in Iraq is what it seems. A quote from an Iraqi man was rattling around in my head … what did he say exactly? Something about, "In Iraq, everything is possible and everything is impossible."

How were we going to train the Iraqi staff and the Iraqi commander if they were going to fire them all the time? Later we were told that General Muhammed, the brigade commander of the NP in our area, tried to reinstate this battalion commander but was overridden by his boss. The replacement was Colonel Ate. Colonel Ate was the guy that all of the policeman liked. He was slightly rotund (most Iraqi commanders are), and he smiled all the time. He had thick black hair and was always in a nice-looking uniform. He seemed to truly care about the policemen's needs and about working with the common people of Sadr City. He was proactive and always checked on his guys out on the operations, checkpoints, and in garrison. He was not very trusting of his subordinates (probably for good reason), and he asked me to give him personal lists of supplies that were given to the battalion so he could personally track them. This was because most of the Iraqi officers and other personnel were very poor and would steal the supplies in a proverbial New York minute. I remember thinking to myself that he was a good guy (although later, we found out that he wasn't).

It would seem to be possible upon first observing the situation in Sadr City to assume that one could locate a non–Jeesh al-Mahdi commander, install him, and have him do good things. This would seem to be the perfect candidate from an American perspective; however, we were not in America. Corruption, bribery, and extortion are normal business practices in Iraq. Add to this the fact that the situation in Sadr City is tenuous, to say the least. JAM apparently controls a large majority of Sadr City. Conventional U.S. forces are not permitted to proceed into these areas in most cases. JAM is alive and well and can make your life hell. You had to deal with them. The common phrase we used is "they get a vote." This means they are such a big factor in wreaking havoc in Iraq that you had to consider them all the time. For the Americans it is easy to sit in a tactical operations center and issue plans and orders to clean out an area. But the Iraqis still have to live in that area after it is cleaned. Fighting the people is the easy part … fighting the ideas is the challenge.

"Sitting at the table" with these people is obviously better than the various firefights and other nasty encounters between coalition forces and the "bad guys." In the case of the National Police in Sadr City, they *must* deal with JAM in many ways that most Americans or American forces are not willing to or are currently unable to do.

Nothing we were taught about Iraq fully prepared us to deal with situations like this. The fact is that this situation, like many others associated with the transition of the security of Iraq, may not even have a solution.

Later on in our tour we moved up to Combat Outpost Hope, and we ended up meeting another Iraqi battalion commander. He was educated and spoke very good English. At times he would speak faster than the interpreter and took over when the interpreter can't handle the military jargon that we were all spitting out in English and in Arabic. His name was Colonel Rasmun, and he was obviously frustrated with the conditions of the place when he arrived and wasted no time getting down to business. He took us on a tour of the place that lasted several hours, in which he pointed out the awful conditions of the place. The *shirta* (policemen) had done all kinds of things to the barracks (which also pissed off the contractors, so they would no longer work on the place). The conditions were pretty bad, lacking power, running water, beds, and simple equipment. The bathrooms had not had running water in months, but that didn't stop the *shirta* from defecating in them. The food storage was horrible. *Shirta* were bathing in the water storage tanks! It took us a few months to work with the contractors and the unit living in the building, but eventually we got everything up to a decent standard of living.

Colonel Rasmun had moved out of the big office and had it converted to a tactical operations center using what little funds the unit had available. He understood how and what types of funding we had available for them, and he immediately quizzed us about it. All I could think at the time was, *Dang, here we go.* Everyone had been having fun with me by telling me that my job as the "loggy" (logistician or supply officer) was going to get easier once we got to Hope. Obviously, that was not going to happen. My job continued to be difficult in supporting the team needs and now the extensive requirements of the National Police. With a nonfunctioning supply system, they were going to need a great deal of assistance with funding. To further highlight the obvious hurdles and challenges we would face, the deputy commanding officer (DCO) of the American unit supporting us spoke to me in the first month or so of my tour. He said to me by phone, "You are not going to be able to fix the Iraqi logistics system for the National Police during your tour here, so go get them some funds and buy them some stuff." I said, "Roger, sir" and hung up the phone. The deputy commanding officer lived and worked at a nasty combat outpost, and little did I know it at the time but I would be on my way to see him a few days later—on what would be our first combat patrol … to the outpost.§

6

The Outpost

"Before me there were no created things, Only eterne, and I eternal last. All hope abandon, ye who enter in!" —Dante's Inferno, *Inscription on the Gates of Hell*

IMMEDIATELY FOLLOWING OUR COMPLETION OF THE PHOENIX ACADEMY—OUR FIRST COMBAT PATROL IN IRAQ

Driving past the barriers and razor wire littered across the four-lane street, it felt as Dante must have felt as he entered the gates of hell. We were still a good distance away from the outpost (at least two city blocks) and could immediately see a massive structure looming in the middle of our view. The highest building in the area, it was covered with black-charred holes from rockets, mortars, bullets, and who knows what else. The holes were strewn with large chunks of cement hanging from the mangled matrix of internal steel rods exposed when rockets blew off pieces of the walls. These pieces of cement littered the area around the outpost, making it difficult to maneuver our vehicles on the grounds as we approached the building. This gave us plenty of time to take in all the sights and sounds of this awful place. The outpost had large weapons and various other electronic equipment and antennae sticking up all over it. It was covered on every corner by sandbagged and fortified gun positions, and it had a medieval look to it that was hard to shake. It was surreal. The dreamy feeling was around us now.

The building was well chosen for its obvious tactical advantages over the area. It was high, it was big, it was solid, and it was set apart from the rest of the neighborhood. It had large parking areas around it. It was obviously a place that you did not approach uninvited … unless you wanted to die. It was the modern-day version of a concept straight out of the Middle Ages—the outpost.

A few years back, I had read *Dante's Inferno* for one of my college courses. It is not an easy book to read, but it is a classic work of literature and was on my list of things to do at the time. A painting in the book was one of Dante Alighieri. In the painting, he was pointing to a procession of sinners who were being led down to the circles of hell. Behind him in the painting is a representation of purgatory. It shows the seven terraces of purgatory in an ominous and towering representation. That painting looked just like this place, both inside and out.

We pulled in to the main gate in our armored vehicles, parked them in a tactical manner, and stepped out into the mid-day sun with our full combat load of equipment on our backs. It was brutal. The heat was easily past 115 degrees Fahrenheit, and it didn't take more than about fifteen seconds to begin to lose precious body fluid out of your sweat glands.

Making our way into the place, we encountered the occupants, who were just as unfriendly as the outpost itself appeared to be. Attacks by armed insurgents with indirect fire from rockets and mortars were a common occurrence here. It's not that the people here (both soldiers and contractors) didn't want to be nice to you; they just had nothing left in them to give. The great suffering the soldiers in this place had endured recently was obvious in their faces.

The soldiers had taken the outpost by force from the enemy in the months prior to our arrival. An infantry battalion and all the advanced firepower they bring to the battlefield took the building from enemy insurgents by force. People died in the process of claiming this building. This wasn't your typical real estate transaction. The bank note on this little property wasn't paid for in cash, it was paid for in blood. We learned that we had caught this unit and its soldiers at the tail end of the worst phase in the unit's time in Iraq. The situation eventually got better for them. The outpost was under constant improvement, but it was slow, and this place needed *lots* of improvement.

The inside was not much better than the outside. The soldiers living and working inside the facility were all pale, severely lacking in the sun's vitamin D. Most people in this place rarely got outside. When they did, they were covered in heavy army equipment, in an armored vehicle. The environment in the outpost was menacing enough without these pale, slumping figures moving around. The depression of knowing that they had to endure a fifteen-month tour in conditions like this had made them numb. It is a scene I will never forget as long as I live.

You could look up from the fountain in the middle of the complex and see them all. At each of the six or seven levels of the facility were people walking around. With railing around the ledges, the center of the facility was an architecturally well-planned foyer. No one here cared about the architecture. It was no longer used for its original purpose and would, over the course of several months, morph into a full-blown military facility. The entire scene was very dark from years of neglect to the electrical systems and lighting. A faint bit of natural light peeked through the opening in the center of the ceiling of the complex (where skylight windows used to be), providing just enough soft illumination to highlight the soldiers' pale faces.

Contractors were working in various places throughout the different levels, installing air-conditioners to rooms with no ceilings and installing lighting fixtures in dank, secluded corners where thirty or more soldiers were piled on top of each other. Master Sergeant Calderon looked at me. I looked at him. Our eyes made contact, and we each received the other's silent message with just a look: "We have got to get out of here."

To add to the strangeness of the situation, almost everything was located inside of the building … including the motor pool, an area normally set up in an outside area to work on vehicles, The mechanics were working on running vehicles, inside the building. The exhaust fumes lingered and caused the smoky haze that the light peaked through. On the other side was a refrigerated truck, parked in front of an area where the food was cooked. The situation we observed is almost beyond words.

With every passing minute, it became more and more apparent that this was not a friendly place for our team to stay or visit. These people were barely caring for themselves. How could they possibly handle supporting us? This was our coalition unit, our sponsor, the battalion that we reported to—incredible.

We were led up to an area where the team prior to us had lived. This was the place where the battalion had forced them to live and operate. It was not conducive to training the National Police, because their headquarters was across town.

We were put in a room and bedded down for the night. Later that evening we were told that a sergeant in the battalion had once been sleeping in that room when a rocket was shot through the wall, chopping both of his legs off. Mortars and rockets impacted the walls and ceilings and exploded all through the night.

The soldiers inside living in the various areas possessed very little of the normal military discipline and cleanliness standards we were all used to. They were living like corralled-up animals in their various areas. It was sad and disgusting.

Fortunately for us, we were only visiting. Our predecessors had convinced the chain of command that we were to temporarily operate out of another combat outpost on the east side of town, thank God. Eventually we moved across town with the National Police battalion that we were supposed to work with at Hope. At the time, this was only the second place we had traveled to during our Iraq tour. Surely, we thought, the other places in Iraq had to be better than this.

The return trip from the outpost was worse than the one that took us to the outpost originally. It was the first time that we had to do this, traveling across Sadr City late in the evening, in the dark, avoiding the main routes as much as possible.

On this particular night, traveling back to our main operating base, we ran into a route clearance team at 4:00 am, with a long convoy behind them. Other normal army units follow behind the route clearance teams. They thought we were crazy. We waved, and they waved back. We kept on our way. Tonight, they were the target, not us. We stuck to our route. We would be the target soon enough.

Later, we were told what the building used to be: it was a shopping mall. §

7

The Firefight

"All night long ... all night ... yeah ... all night long"—Lionel Ritchie, "All Night Long"

FOUR MONTHS IN IRAQ—COMBAT MISSION WITH IRAQI NATIONAL POLICE

Humming nervously the Lionel Ritchie song "All Night Long," I waited for the lights on the city block to turn off. The lights had only been on for about five minutes, and we had been taking fire from almost every direction during those long, five minutes. At the time, we thought the enemy was harassing us by turning on and off the generator that provides power to the block. The enemy had engaged us with AK-47 rifle fire twice already, and it was as if a video game would start each time the lights went off. Maybe they did not realize that it was better for us to be in complete darkness. With all of the tools at our disposal, we literally "owned the night."

Once the lights were off, we could see clearly the surrounding area to determine where the enemy was.

Our truck was in the right side lane, facing south, and it was probably around 2:00 am or so by this time. My job was to drive an armored Humvee with the noncommissioned officer in charge of the infantry team attached to us for security.. Our truck had the .50-caliber machine gun, or the "ma deuce," as it is commonly referred to. We were facing the same direction as a Stryker vehicle from the Quick Reaction Force (QRF). The QRF is on call. They respond as directed to units in the area to provide assistance and extra firepower. It is a great feeling when they show up. These same guys had responded to our call for assistance earlier in the evening. My heart was pounding so hard in my chest that I could almost feel it hitting the inside of my flak vest. The young private manning the weapon, our vehicle's gunner, had just fired several nine-round bursts on the .50-caliber machine gun in the direction that we were taking fire from. The large, smoking-hot, five-inch-long shell casings were raining down on us inside of the vehicle. I watched in horror through the bulletproof glass as an incoming round hit the front of our vehicle.

Two AH-64 helicopters, a couple of F-16 fixed-wing aircraft, and about four or five Stryker vehicles were assisting us while this was going on. We suspected that we were going to be hit this evening, but no one expected to be attacked on such a scale. We were definitely at risk, but there was an overwhelming feeling of security from all the coordinated efforts of the various elements participating in this armed response. In my years of military service, I had seen displays of combat power in tactical exercises and a battle in Desert Storm. Never had I personally witnessed the execution of such awesome force as this.

The previous night we were engaged in a short firefight. We suspect that some of the National Police that accompany General Muhammed, the National Police brigade commander, may have been involved. Most of that first night was uneventful until late in the morning. We had been naming off movies on the radio to keep ourselves awake. It was a funny and easy game where you name a movie and then the next truck/team had to come up with the name of a movie that starts with the last letter of the movie that you had just mentioned. If you had a movie with a double-letter name (such as Dare Devil) then the order reversed back to the previous truck. We had been playing the game for hours when a call came over the radio: "This is Whitebird 3, enemy forces are currently massing north of your area for an attack ... we are sending the quick reaction force to your position." Holy Shit! Our situation had just gotten very serious, very quickly.

We had personnel outside of the vehicles who were checking on the status of the mission when the bullets started flying. We did a pickup drill at that point. A pickup drill is when all the team vehicles go to the location where your dismounted personnel are and pick them up while maintaining security with the vehicles. Our dismount (person outside vehicle) was the security sergeant, and he said that as he was running to the vehicle he heard several rounds *swoosh* by his head, so he immediately ducked down behind the bumper of the vehicle. After we got him inside the vehicle, we set up another perimeter using the vehicles with all personnel inside them. The QRF was with us on this night, but they were not with us in our perimeter as they had been on the previous evening. The helicopters were circling overhead, and everyone was talking on the net to the team chief, who was the senior person on the ground. We wrapped things up and eventually returned to our base of operations. Little did we know that we would again be working with the QRF and the helicopters the next night.

Everyone on the team was nervous when we started out that second evening, but I did not feel particularly overwhelmed. We were on an extended mission advising the National Police to provide security and barrier escorts to improve fortified checkpoints throughout Sadr City. (Jeesh-Al-Mahdi were everywhere in the area we were going, as this is where they lived and operated out of.) The engagement by enemy forces on the previous night's mission forced us to reconcile some issues for this evening's mission and adjust our plan.

Our missions started out the same each night, and we were worried about setting discernable patterns. Tonight, we would do things differently, both in how we maneuvered to the objective and how we secured it. I was very happy that our team chief was a smart person. He learned from his mistakes and made adjustments when necessary. This was the most important attribute that he could have possibly brought to the team, in my opinion.

We left about the time it got dark, with thirteen or fourteen total civilian flatbed eighteen-wheel trucks filled with ten-foot-tall cement barriers and several crane trucks. In addition, we had about four or five NP trucks and our own compliment of armored vehicles. Tonight, we did not disperse ourselves throughout the convoy as we had done on previous missions.

The communication with the National Police was almost impossible because of the language barrier and their nonsecure communications. We briefed their Lieutenant Allah, an extremely squared away officer (who is also the battalion maintenance officer) and then called him occasionally through our interpreter, who carried one of the National Police handheld radios. We had to shut the electronic equipment off for the radio to work, so we did not do it very often. We were very skeptical of the police this evening. Some of us on the team suspected that some of the National Police had fired their weapons at us the previous night. Therefore, our vehicles traveled together tonight.

"Why did I join the army?" I was wondering this to myself aloud (again). How can one be with an organization for so many years and still ask himself this question? Over the years, the reasons had changed, with age and rank. This made me think back to my first conversation with an army recruiter so long ago, when he had said, "Can you see yourself being airborne and going on the adventure of your lifetime?" Wow! If this was not an adventure of a lifetime, then what could possibly top this?

We reached the emplacement site at an ungodly hour of the morning and then established a security perimeter with our vehicles. The National Policemen were somewhat confused by the way that we arrayed our vehicles, but they were a wildcard in this situation. We later learned that although we thought Lieutenant Allah was in charge of the NPs (National Police) and the emplacement, in fact he was not. Later that same evening, an Iraqi captain and an Iraqi major from another NP battalion showed up in the middle of the firefight, knocking on our Humvee's window. They were trying to make contact with us about the status of the operation.

We did not acknowledge him because of recent deceptions by the enemy using captured uniforms. Jeesh al-Mahdi had captured the blue, computer-patterned uniforms used by the NP and used them to attack a checkpoint at a military facility. We had no way to confirm who they were and had never met them before.

The events of the evening were amazing in every respect. However, the most amazing thing of the entire evening was the fact that the drivers and crane operators continued to work the entire evening! They were placing humongous cement barriers. We had contact from the enemy altogether about five or six times over the course of a four-hour period, and the crane operators never stopped working! Our focus was completely on the firefight. During the lulls in the fighting, we wondered what was going on with the barrier emplacement.

Hats off to those people. Maybe they were not at risk as much as initially thought, but the rounds were flying everywhere, so they had to be at some risk. Two nights ago, we had all been sitting around some trucks, eating an Iraqi meal with all the Iraqi drivers and operators, so they were familiar to me. It was the first time I had ever tried to use my Iraqi interaction skills on my own. My brief attempts at communication with the Iraqi's in Arabic went a long way.

After emplacing the security perimeter with our vehicles, it was not long before we began to take fire. *A little worm on a big hook*, I thought. We are a small but extremely well equipped and well-armed team, and we proved to ourselves that we could hold an area with some assistance. Although the entire incident scared the shit out of me, at the time I never doubted that we were in complete control of the situation. Our vehicle smelled of the burnt gunpowder from the machine gun rounds fired. The occupants in our vehicle were pumped up and excited. The dreamy feeling surrounded us. The following is an edited portion of a summary of the incident and gives a good idea of what we encountered:

"We reported the contact to our higher headquarters, and this is how we had helicopter support so quickly. The F-16s were able to engage the enemy forces in contact with the unit. After the fixed-wing attack, the enemy broke contact. During the lull in the battle we identified three enemy dead from the ground engagement of one Stryker vehicle and one Humvee. A little after 0100, another enemy insurgent tried to recover an RPG [rocket-propelled grenade] from the dead bodies of the enemy, and we engaged and killed him. For the next forty-five minutes we remained in contact from three different directions. At about 0230, enemy forces resumed their attack. Shortly thereafter, we once again received helicopter support. The helicopters engaged the enemy from the air, killing two more enemies. At this point, we had an F-18 aircraft get in on the fight with us, also support and another American platoon showed up to assist. Then the enemy broke contact."

The sound of the machine gun coming from the aircraft was loud and a little scary. It sounds like a humongous, fifty-foot chainsaw revving highly inside a barrel into a microphone right into your ear. *Whaaoopp!* The machine gun shot out bursts of thirty-millimeter rounds at who knows how many rounds per second. The crackling of reports was coming over the radio, but we were not getting everything on the net because the team chief's vehicle traffic had to be relayed to us from another vehicle. We had to get a loaner vehicle the night before due to transmission problems in one of our trucks, so our radio system was different from the others. The security NCO was an experienced combat veteran with tours in Fallujah and Afghanistan. He knew what he was doing. Our gunner was well trained and performing superbly. Doc was the third person in my vehicle, and he was stirred up from all the night's activities. Doc was a good medic and a good shot; I was glad he was in the vehicle with us.

The reports we were getting in our vehicle sounded something like this: "We are taking fire … someone is shooting at us!" We had four people in our truck, and we all screamed in unison at the top of our lungs, *"Shoot back!"* Again came the same reports of taking fire, of enemy combatants running around the hasty perimeter. Again we would scream, *"Shoot back!"* all in unison. It was amazing. You never really know people's reactions to a combat situation until it actually happens to you.

I was a little numb from the flow of adrenaline going through my veins. As the adrenaline high began to wear off, time began to speed up again. I noticed more and more of the many things going on around me: the flicking of the infrared strobe coming from the vehicle behind us, the AK-47 fire coming from the mosque and apartments to our left, the .50-caliber machine gun on the Stryker engaging shooters from the mosque, the radio traffic about counting the enemy dead bodies, and the aircraft flying around us, the "clink, clink" of rounds hitting. *"Swoosh!"* Something fired (or misfired) near our vehicle, and the fixed-wing aircraft fired a hundred meters ahead of us with a type of spinning cannon that used thirty-millimeter rounds.

Fixed checkpoints like the ones we were making are a pariah in this area to most Americans. The ultimate goal here for the Iraqis is to have a large, cement-laden security checkpoint to assist the police with checking and securing the area. However, on most occasions you drive up to one of these checkpoints and find one person awake, waving cars through, and the rest of them are sleeping, bathing, or eating. The previous team leader and senior officers in the Brigade Combat Team warned us when we first arrived that the checkpoints are worthless—worthless because the Jeesh Al-Mahdi will roll up with a trunk full of dead bodies and tell the person operating the checkpoint that if he does not let them through the same thing will happen to his family; worthless because they take an extensive use of human resources to run them, and this limits the available forces that you have to go out and actually conduct operations, raids, and other policing.

As if to prove that this is true, we were once driving down one of the main streets in Sadr City when from out of the corner of my eye I saw something—a car full of well-dressed men in an extremely nice, new Mercedes (most probably they were Jeesh Al-Mahdi). One of them was holding a child who looked to be about the same age as my son at the time. He held the boy up in the air by one hand and one leg while putting him in the car's trunk. The boy was crying, screaming, and squirming to free himself. The large, well-dressed Iraqi man placing the boy in the trunk had no emotion on his face. It was as if he was possessed. The relatives of the boy were nearby and were screaming and crying. The scene made me sick to my stomach. I couldn't do anything. It was only three seconds as I drove past in my armored Humvee. Our convoy was at risk, and we could not stop here. It is the longest, most vivid three-second memory that plays over and over in my head. The boy was fighting and squirming … I hope he is okay, but I will always have to wonder. This vision is so stuck in my mind that I cannot forget it. Systematic ethnic cleansing between the Shia and the Sunni was going on in force in this area during this time.

Several firefights later, we were now battle tested. and we had passed the test. We had used our training, experience, and technology to best an enemy force and accomplish a mission while under attack from rifles and rocket-propelled grenades.

When you come out of an experience like this, you never know whether to tell your loved ones back on the home front. If you tell them too much, they will worry all the time, and you risk them shutting down on you. Things are very hard with them back home, too … sometimes harder. §

8

The Home Front

"The hardest thing that you will ever do as a soldier ... is just to go home and live a normal life"—U.S. Army instructor

FOUR MONTHS IN IRAQ—UP TO THIS POINT. THIS BOOK HAD ONLY EXISTED IN MY NOTEBOOK, DISCUSSIONS WITH FRIENDS AND FAMILY, AND E-MAILS HOME

It is easy to pass away the many months of a long deployment doing various things to keep your mind occupied, but eventually the war wears you down. It stresses you out. Everyone is susceptible. Stress does not come out when you want it to. It comes out when you are not prepared for it. You internalize things, and your body and your mind put up various defense mechanisms to help you deal with the things that you see, things that human beings are not supposed to see—ugly things ... things I will leave to your imagination. All soldiers know this. It can be studied and analyzed, but somehow society never seems to really get it. War changes people.

All you can really do about it is understand that you are different. This lesson I have learned several times. You don't feel the same when you are at home, but you are expected to be the same person you were when you left home. It's the "Rip Van Winkle" effect: If you can, recall the story of the guy who was in a deep sleep and woke up many years later. You want things to be the same, you want to make up for lost time, you want a lot … and so do the loved ones that you left behind. The truth is, they suffer too.

Your family worries about you all the time, even when you are sleeping safely on a secure forward operating base with no worries. You are out of range of any mortars, with more than 150 armed personnel guarding the perimeter, and still they worry. My family is a part of me and who I am. Without them, I feel lost. Any soldier who is also a family man deals with this hell all the time.

When I returned from my first tour in OIF 1 (Operation Iraqi Freedom—deployment number one), I knew, like many other army leaders, that we would be back. We had left so much undone. So many questions existed that we knew we would have to come back. It wasn't a question of if, it was a question of when. This has haunted me all the way up to when I arrived once again in Iraq. Never would I have imagined that I would be doing what I was today, but nevertheless it was a relief: the strange relief of knowing that I didn't have to worry about coming back anymore, because I was here. Confusing, isn't it? Not to a soldier. Ask them, and they will tell you about the feeling. The military briefs you about this feeling before you go home on leave and before you return home after you are done with your tour. It is called guilt, the guilt you feel because you are living a good life when others no longer can. My mind wanders back home as I sit and write these words.

The barefoot little girl standing in a burning trash dump (as big as my entire neighborhood back home) on the side of the road makes me think about my little girl. My little girl wants to marry me when I get home, as all young girls do as they figure out life and how to live it. All I can think is that somehow I have to get home to my family. I don't want to be in this place and neither do the people here, I suspect.

The stresses of returning to a "normal" life are something most people wouldn't realize. But it is there. Soldiers go through this frequently. My way of thinking about it is this: I think of the happiest moments that I can remember as a child with my father and I try to do those things with my kids as much as I can.

In my discussions with other team members, one of the common things we have with our families are the difficulties in communicating with our family members. It is very hard to listen to your wife when she talks about a promotion or the kids starting school when all you can think about is war—blood, bullets, burnt metal scraps on the road.

Soldiers carry around a lot of baggage, figuratively and literally. Emotionally, you carry around the scars and the pain from the child within us all who wants to go back home to mom so she can make everything alright.

My wife and family never understood this. When I spent time working on my car, getting lost in the technicalities, the feeling would go away. It was pure therapy to deal with the anxiety. In retrospect, I should have spent more time with them.

I did spend many joyous times with my wife and children in the months before I left, probably more than I had in the last year prior to that: We went to the park, we went to the Chuck-e-Cheese amusement center, we went to the movies. We spent quality time. Meanwhile, I worried that I was not acting normal enough.

Ultimately, it is the happiest things in your life that you use to fight this crazy battle in your head. You try to balance it out. Doesn't that make sense? If you've seen so much unhappiness, shouldn't you try to make things in your life as happy as you can? Soldiers carry around a lot of that baggage.

Speaking of baggage, the home front provided our team with lifesaving supplies while we were in Iraq—kids' backpacks. Yes, backpacks. This was our little way of balancing things out in Iraq with the help of those on the home front in the United States. In Sadr City, one of the few actual normal schools in the entire area was a school for young girls. The school was pitiful, but it represented the future to so many people to include the young girls who walk the dangerous war-torn streets of Sadr City every day to attend classes at that school. Basic school supplies and clothes for the children were nonexistent. Most of them didn't even have shoes.

My wife teamed up with a good friend and some other folks from her work place to package up as many backpacks and school supplies for the young girls as they possibly could. Our friend (I'll call her "Saint Mary") provided boxes and boxes full of these supplies and backpacks at her own expense to us in Iraq. She did not stop with one or two shipments, either; she kept sending supplies over the months. These backpacks and supplies kept us alive and helped us to cement our relationship with the Iraqis in many ways. That may sound surprising, but they did. Those backpacks bridged the gap for us with our Iraqi unit. We gave them the supplies, and they gave them to the school. This worked well culturally with the Iraqis because it helped in our bonding and relationships to go beyond the military training and issues we dealt with on a day-to-day basis. Also, these were highly prized items to them because they were pricey and difficult to obtain in Iraq.

We went beyond our day-to-day typical worries about which Iraqi soldier was secretly working with Jeesh Al-Mahdi. Many of them *were* working with Jeesh Al-Mahdi, but it is not what they really wanted. Iraq is a desperate place, and necessity takes on a completely new meaning when added to desperation. The Iraqis became our friends. We became human to them. Our long-standing fears about being killed while living and working with the Iraqis melted away over this time. The Iraqis protected us, and we protected them.

My mom and her church and her work place sent us many items over those months also, highly appreciated items. I sent my mom a photo once, and I never thought about it again after that. I was waiting at a helipad for a helicopter to arrive and take us to our combat outpost. After my return from Iraq, my mom told me that the photo was passed around her office and was printed and pasted on many computer desktops. They prayed for me and for the team. Practically the whole office had the photo up, and I never knew about it. I became *their* soldier. They wanted to help us somehow, more than just the supplies. They wanted a face, and a name and a person to relate to about this war. My photo became that link. I was their soldier.

The funny thing about this was the way that they wanted to be a part of the war somehow, but I desperately did not. I was shocked, speaking to a Vietnam veteran who said these words prior to me leaving for Iraq. He said to me, "I've had my war … this is your war … you'll figure it out." My war? How could this be my war? I didn't start it. I don't want to go to it. I don't want to kill anyone. "This is your war. You'll figure it out." So this is my war. At the time, I did not know what the Vietnam vet was talking about. I was corresponding with him to get some parts for my classic car on eBay. He had been an advisor in Vietnam, and I was asking for his advice about being on a transition team. At the time, before my deployment, it was not personal to me. It is personal now. I didn't realize it at the time, but he had just taught me my first lesson about being on a transition team. Overall, the only ones who can truly understand all of it are the people on your left and right on your team. The friends, family, and coworkers on the home front truly play the most important role of all: they are what you are fighting for. You are *their* soldier.

Besides just documenting the team's adventures, what I really wanted to do was share my experiences with others who need to hear it. §

9

The First One Hundred Days

> "Complacency is the worst killer."—U.S. Army instructor

We had made it. We were all still alive and still in Iraq. In our first one hundred days. we experienced explosively formed penetrators, improvised explosive devices, survived enemy mortars, faced enemy gunfire; we earned our combat action badges, combat infantry badges, and combat medic badges five times over. Having passed the one hundred–day mark, your percentage rate of survival dramatically increases. The first one hundred days is a critical time for learning and soaking up the lessons of those who have come before you. There are many things to learn for soldiers of all experience levels, both the new and old soldiers. War has changed. The army has changed. Iraq has changed.

As an institution, the army has been in Iraq so long that it is getting hard to remember what it was like back in 2003's Operation Iraqi Freedom 1. Wars like Bosnia, Somalia, or even Desert Storm were ages ago, and the lessons from them seem forgotten, for the most part.

Getting through (alive) your first couple of months in Iraq is actually easy, if you are one of the typical soldiers who lives and works in Iraq. We call them "fobbits" (a play on the words *hobbit* and *fob*). Most transition teams are not what you would consider fobbits. Our team spent a great deal of time outside the wire of the operating base or outpost. We rolled outside the wire frequently, both at night and during the day with minimal guidance and a lot of coordination. We drove our sand-covered, bullet-riddled, ten-thousand-pound armored vehicles in small convoys that invited disaster. The blow-off valve from the turbo on the massive motors makes an impressive sound when you are driving around the city. We carried enough firepower to take down anything we encountered. In addition, if we could not handle it, we had friends in combat units that followed us in the air and on the ground, and they were itching to use their toys.

Our team had an amazing amount of brainpower, ability, and experience, with senior sergeants and commissioned officers, all specialized in their job and using their fullest abilities. The main areas covered here relate directly to many of the items in the U.S. Army's book, *The First 100 Days.* If used to their fullest abilities, one can overcome all the potential hazards that the army writes about. To explain I will highlight the areas of risk, physical fitness, maintenance, battle rhythm, intelligence, training, pre-combat checks and inspections, hand receipts and funding, soldier experience, and leadership.

Risk

The first one hundred days is a critical time in a soldier's life, when the chances of survival in combat are low. During the first one hundred days, you are essentially so new and inexperienced that this is a highly likely time when inexperienced soldiers will be killed or injured. In some form or another, our team encountered extreme adversity in combat and came out of it with only some minor injuries. This is proof that risk can be managed in combat. Making sound decisions and reviewing intelligence data is critical. Knowing where and why and who is trying to get you helps to avoid unnecessary risk. We, as a team, have made mistakes, and we have made poor decisions. However, when we do make a bad call, we make it together and we follow our rule: If the first truck takes the wrong turn, *you all take the wrong turn!*

We operated as a single, effective, well-tuned unit. Overall, there was an understanding among the majority of the team not only to do well at your assigned task, but to try to do it even better. We were not the same people or the same team that left Fort Riley a few months ago. When you get back to base, you let off steam, you blow off some small tasks, and you talk about the hardships of the patrols and the missions. You do not do this when you are out on the road, out on mission. You focus, you get into the "zone," and you stay there, sometimes for eight to ten hours or more. It is exhausting but necessary. This exhaustion is a good point to lead us into the next major issue, fitness.

Physical Fitness

Physical fitness, when you can fit it in, helps you to deal with the stress and exhaustion. You won't always be able to do it in combat.

As a whole, we had a fit team and most of us took it seriously. My combat load when we weighed in to get on the airplane to come to Iraq was 293 pounds. That was my body, my military equipment on my body (body armor and small attachments), and a laptop bag. I weigh 185 pounds, soaking wet. The point is, you have to be physically fit to be a soldier, now more than ever. Your body eventually adjusts to the amount of weight you carry, and the extreme heat you endure, but I have never completely gotten used to it. Hydration is critical and must be monitored all the time. It is so easy to dehydrate in 115-degree heat with carrying all this weight while doing heavy duties. Once you are behind on drinking water, you won't catch up while out on a patrol. I now have flat feet and bad knees—I wonder why? (Note the sarcasm,)

Maintenance

On several occasions, my logistician duties required me to stay back from patrol to coordinate support for the team. A great deal of the issues our team dealt with were logistics related, either for the team or for the NP. Every person I met in briefings, in the chain of command, or in partner units, the first thing they usually would say is, "Who is your logistics guy? He has a huge task ahead of him." The lesson learned here is that the logistics guy better be "on his game" (well prepared for his duties) or the whole team is going to suffer.

After we relieved the previous team, we immediately sought out a friend of mine in BIAP (Baghdad International Airport) who was tied in to the maintenance contracts at Camp Victory. At the time, our vehicles would barely move. All the turbochargers in the vehicles we inherited were blown. This was only one issue with the vehicles (but a major one). Two of the vehicles needed either a completely new engine or a new engine and a new transmission. Many of the vehicles were missing mounts and had major suspension problems. These vehicles live a hard life in combat and are usually toast within six months without extensive maintenance.

I flew down by helicopter and coordinated the arrival of my team and our vehicles to conduct a refurbishment and refit of the vehicles. We spent two weeks at this installation while civilian contractors poured over our vehicles and changed turbochargers, engines, transmissions, radio parts, and various other issues. Within two months, we were already starting to see wear from the road time. The desert is brutal on the vehicles, and they required constant maintenance. The lesson learned here is to plan for this when you arrive because you never know what the team you replace is going to hand to you.

This time spent was one of the most important things that we had done to date. It directly attributed to saving our lives on a few occasions when we needed the vehicles to perform at their best.

Battle Rhythm

Another key task that we accomplished was to set a regular battle rhythm (schedule). We dedicated a day (mission dictating) where we did nothing but maintenance. We also always tried to have a "down day" prior to missions (if we could) to maintain ourselves. When you are working seven days a week for a year in combat, this is critical. This small bit of rest kept us tuned up like our vehicles and allowed us to get ourselves prepared for the eight to twelve hours of focus required to perform our various missions. (Believe me, those missions were usually crazy).

Intelligence

Our intelligence people really know their stuff. Our intel officer spent an hour or two in the mornings reviewing intelligence updates and meeting with other intel folks to get updates on our routes and missions. He actually analyzed the data and provided the commander with options and recommendations. Usually, it is just the typical stuff, such as this route is red and that one is black. However, sometimes we really got some updates that blew our minds and completely changed the plan. On several occasions, this saved our lives. On one particular occasion we decided at the last minute to take a different route and be a little bit unpredictable. As we left the forward operating base, we were following a convoy, which waved at us and kept going straight down the road, while we didn't. We took a left to take a longer route than we normally would have. Several miles away, we heard a large explosion and saw a large cloud of smoke. That convoy was hit with an explosive device. If we had followed them, we most likely would have been hit. The flexibility to change the plan is a key point.

Be flexible. Everything changes all the time on transition teams. You have to understand the way things are working around you. We were driving the Iraqis to be more proactive and to lead more missions. You are not going to get as much notice that you would like to have prior to missions. You have to do drills and pre-combat inspections to be prepared and ready to go at a moment's notice. You have to have a sign-out board and radios and know where everyone is at all times.

Battle Drills and Pre-combat Inspections

While we were training at Fort Riley, we did a lot of work on battle drills (rehearsals) and we continued to do this in an informal manner (we seemed to do everything that way; that is what small team dynamics is like). In hindsight, we could have worked more on some standard operating procedures and checklists. Personally, some of the less combat-experienced guys like me (I only had two previous combat tours, whereas some of our guys had four and five combat tours in "actual" combat firefights) need a little tutoring in some areas that are second nature to the more experienced guys.

Hand Receipts and Funding

It takes a constant effort to keep track of the property book items. We moved around so much that it was difficult to assign property and tasks to people on the team. In addition, most of the logistics work was done in my spare time. You have to have a thorough understanding of property, because Iraq does not really operate as it used to.

A few years ago, you could literally write-off losses due to battle loss and very few people would question you. Now, almost everything is on the hand receipt and accounted for, even items that you normally would not put on the hand receipt in a company command in the United States. This is good business practice, but war is not a business. The impracticalities of the administration and accounting for these items in combat was my constant headache.

We were so far away from supply nodes in central Baghdad we had to purchase supplies to sustain us. The previous team did a good job of leaving us with nothing, so we spent our first two month's worth of money getting basic supplies. Learning the system when you first arrive is a task that the outgoing team should show you. It can be challenging to work the funding documents through all the various staff elements to get the funding. You have to stay on top of this stuff.

Experience of Noncommissioned Officers

Listen to your noncommissioned officers—they have vast experience. We are lucky enough to have received a few of the army's finest senior noncommissioned officers. The advice that they brought to the table had saved our butts numerous times. The things they have to say are not always what you want to hear but usually it is what you need to hear. We, as a team, collectively recognized this, and most of us listened with ears wide open when they spoke.

Team Chief/Leadership

Our team chief admittedly had no Iraq combat experience coming in to this tour. You would not know it now. He spent endless hours in conversations with his senior sergeants and had to bend like a willow tree on many issues to the recommendations of his team. However, he has done well. He was also able to use the team's various strengths and weaknesses toward the greater good of the team. This is critical to your survival as a transition team because you are so small.

In many ways our team is autonomous (a good thing and a bad thing), but we were still "in the net." Many times, we had three different bosses and sometimes none. We had the brigade team, the combat battalion, and the deputy commanding officer of the brigade usually all giving us guidance. You think because you do not hear from anyone for long periods of time that you are all alone sometimes.

In the end, one learns many small things in the first few months, and the best advice I can provide is to keep a diary or account in your green book and write them down. My first green book notebook/diary was like a standard operating procedure book for me and captured the rest of our experiences. Hopefully, someone else can learn something from our experiences. §

10

Looking for Hope

> "Therefore take up the whole armor of God, that you may be able to withstand in the evil day, … having fastened on the belt of truth, and having put on the breastplate of righteousness, … the shield of faith … the helmet of salvation … and the sword of the spirit, which is the word of God."—Ephesians 6:10–20, ESV

MONTH FIVE—CONVOY TO COMBAT OUTPOST HOPE. WE WERE MOVING TO LIVE WITH OUR COUNTERPART IRAQI BATTALION.

The convoy was hit by a large and very powerful explosion. *Boom!* Black smoke billowed up hundreds of feet into the air. Later, after we had made it to our destination, we learned that the convoy was hit by an EFP. It blew heavy plates of armor off of a Bradley tank, which is not an easy thing to do. It was an extremely loud explosion, and the pressure change from the shock wave immediately hurt my ears like a dull earache. I later went to a medic about the ear pain and was told it is similar to the air pressure change on an airplane and there was nothing they could do about it. Luckily, my eardrums did not tear or burst.

The team chief was running out of captains, with all the taskings and problems on that given day. He needed a captain to serve as patrol leader for our team, and today I was that captain. My task was to serve as the convoy patrol leader for our team vehicles. On our usual patrols, this was a more complicated task. Considering that this convoy already had a convoy commander, it wasn't too difficult a task for me on this occasion. It was a convoy of MTT teams, explosive ordnance disposal teams, some logistics guys driving some trucks, and a few tanks. That was our convoy.

The American unit running the convoy was unimpressive. But we had no other choice, so we had to go with them. The unit in charge did no rehearsals, the details of the convoy were sketchy, the brief to the drivers and assistant drivers didn't happen, many vehicles were unequipped with electronic counter devices, there was too much horsing around on the radio, there was no intelligence update or call in to the operations center, the medical evacuation/casualty evacuation plan was weak, no special teams of any kind were identified, no one knew where the medic was located: overall, it was all very sloppy. The information we got about the convoy prior to departing was similar to this:

"The checkpoint halfway through the route [the most dangerous one in Iraq] will be secured by five Bradley tanks [it wasn't], you will have air cover from Apache helicopters [they weren't there], and you will have another section of tanks when you take the final turn to Hope [they also weren't there]."

My job in the vehicle really just boiled down to keeping tabs on everything that was going on with the radio, keeping control of my gunner and driver, and watching for anything out of the ordinary. My driver was new to the team and had never driven the armored Humvee before in our formation. In my mind, I was trying to keep awareness of exactly where I was on the map as I had been taught (just in case I had to call in a medical evacuation).

The convoy was actually hit by an explosive device twice as we progressed on our route. The first explosion came across the radio as an improvised explosive device. "Yikes," I said to myself under my breath. We heard a slight, muffled "pop" sound that was a mile or two away, but it didn't register with us at the time that it was an explosion. The explosion was right along the route we were currently headed on, and it had just hit a convoy twenty minutes ahead of us (ironically, the explosive ordnance disposal guys got hit). The radio traffic was all over the place talking about vehicle speeds, asking which side of the road to travel on, getting other updates. I was trying to listen to two different radio nets, control the driver, and scream at the gunner to keep people away. The convoy commander and serial commander were discussing on the radio net the absence of any assistance. The other companies were supposed to be securing the hot spots along our route. They were also talking about the fact that we were now entering what they termed "Indian country," meaning, once we got past this next checkpoint, things would get very dangerous. And then—*Boom!*

The explosion instantly sent a black cloud of smoke at least a hundred feet in the air! The shock wave from the blast hurt my ears. My adrenaline was flowing again. It took a few seconds to realize that the vehicle ahead of us was hit. (Remember, everything seems to happen in slow motion when you are in an attack.) We saw pieces of flying metal and watched three or four Iraqi civilian guys run off to the right side of the road while another group ran off to the left side of the road. We could not engage the civilians with our weapons because of the rules of engagement. No one had seen who had triggered the explosive. It could have been anyone around the area, and the area was covered with civilians. The road was narrow, and my guess was that it was probably a command-wire detonated blast. Months later, one of the explosive ordinance disposal guys gave me a piece of the copper shrapnel from the EFP device that had exploded in front of us. As he handed me the little piece of copper, I asked him about his driver, and he said that the man was still in the hospital at Walter Reed. The explosion had hit him in his leg, destroyed his hearing, and peppered his face with copper. In addition, the shock of the blast had given him a severe case of post-traumatic stress disorder (PTSD). But he was alive. Better to be alive, I thought to myself.

The area was supposed to have been secured by some tanks from one of the American companies or troops, but they weren't there, and that wasn't all. The guys that were supposed to secure the checkpoint following this area weren't present either. The explosion was on the same side of the road as the one that had happened to the previous convoy. It was a pile of dirt on the southern lane of a small highway, and we were traveling against traffic. The area should have been secured by tanks before we arrived, and we should have not been on that side of the road. We should have had air support.

At least we had tanks. Without them, it would be committing suicide on this route. It has been called "the most dangerous route in Iraq" by several guys I've spoken with who travel all over Iraq. "EFP alley" was one of the location's descriptions that I had heard used on a couple of occasions.

Amazingly, the tank made it with us on the route the rest of the way. It was too dangerous to stop, so the tank crept along and stayed with us until we finished the mission. Later, we passed the tank as we came in the gate, and I was able to see the damage that it had sustained. "That was an EFP," I thought to myself. At the time everyone thought that it was an improvised explosive device (IED). I remembered from training what the photos looked like for both IEDs and EFPs. Several silver dollar–sized holes were present with a copper color surrounding them. It was definitely an EFP, a tube-shaped device that uses a shape charge of explosives inside of a tube to blast out molten copper that is shaped by the charge into a form of projectile. It is the poor man's solution to modern day guerilla tactics. We would learn in the coming months that Iraqis were paid cash based on successful explosions and sniper attacks in which Americans were killed, preferably on video so that this could be shown later on the Internet.

My ears rang much louder than they did before I came to Iraq, but at least I was alive. In Iraq, one must be acutely aware of the surroundings. Eat with them, they say; Iraqis never kill anyone that they eat with. Well, at least I remembered that from my training at Fort Riley.

Emotions run deep with experiences like these and should not be taken lightly. There is a freedom that comes with sharing these thoughts freedom that someone might understand why your mind brings you back to that same moment all the time, even when it shouldn't. Why it is burned in your mind so vividly, like a branding iron? Why can't you forget it … ever. §

11

The Heroes

> "Fight what's wrong to prove what's right, remember the heroes who fight for the right to choose, remember the heroes—we've all got a lot to lose."—Sammy Hagar, *"Remember the Heroes"*

MONTH FIVE, SADR CITY, IRAQ, ON PATROL IN THE MULHALLAHS

This is not a happy story, but it is a heroic one. It is also a typical story of the situations young soldiers deal with on a daily basis in Iraq. These twenty-something-year-old soldiers are the ones who you see now in the United States at military medical facilities recovering and awaiting decisions about their eventual military discharge. They walk around with horrible facial wounds, damaged or missing limbs (primarily on the right side), hearing aids, extensive burns, and other injuries. The soldiers are hard to look at and even harder to talk to, because you are a soldier, they are a reminder of your own potential fate.

The typical American doesn't usually see how these things happen to these soldiers. Well, this is how it happens. I assure you, this story is very representative of how these soldiers receive these injuries. The story begins with a couple of thugs who get on the Internet and download instructions to make an EFP. Sometimes Iranians give these thugs some specially made supplies, and they sit in a garage or a house and build this crazy, homemade explosive device. Then, an American patrol goes out and is exposed in a hostile area, and they are sometimes blown up by these explosives.

The soldiers are out and about so that they can send a message. The message is, "We (the U.S. and Iraqi forces) are here, driving around, and we are okay. You are safe." Around the time of this incident, this story was talked about for several months off and on between the infantry guys and the guys on our team before I wrote up this account.

It was a typical patrol, in which several U.S. vehicles and a couple of NP vehicles were looking for sites from which the bad guys would shoot mortars at us. The soldiers and policemen were traveling around in trucks and Humvees. The patrol had information from higher headquarters to be on the lookout for a specific suspicious vehicle, so they were trying to find this vehicle. Captain Black was the U.S. Army advisor to the Iraqi NP riding along on the patrol.

It was early afternoon, at the end of the patrol. Finishing the search of northern Sadr City, they got a call over the radio from the security station. A suspicious truck with speakers on it was blaring some kind of message. Captain Black's intelligence officer brain was kicking in now. Running over the scenarios in his head, he wondered what it could be, based on the intelligence information that he had read that morning. The description of the truck was a blue Kia, driven by one man, with speakers in its bed. It took only about five minutes to get to the spot where the truck was located.

The night before the patrol, Captain Black had had a very vivid dream. The dream was of the team getting hit by an IED. This dream was so real that he could actually feel in the dream getting hit by the explosive device and see the faces of people about to be burned. He woke up and said to himself, "Boy, I hope that doesn't happen today." He was afraid to go on patrol that day.

His gut told him that the street he was on was evil, and that it lived, and breathed, and wanted to kill us. (I've had a similar feeling—Iraq will do that to you.) As the advisor, you had little control over where the patrol was going. Your input to the situation was purely advisory, and neither side (the U.S. or Iraqi) seemed to listen. It felt like being a helpless animal stuck in a hot oven, scratching at the door to get out.

About an hour or so into the patrol, Captain Black felt and heard a horrendous sound much as he had in the dream. The sheer force of an IED exploding threw him forward against the door and window, nailing his arm and upper body there. An EFP struck the rear vehicle in the convoy and blew an extremely large hole in the vehicle, a hole that was big enough for the soldiers to crawl through it—yep, they had to crawl out of the hole. The blast had rendered the five hundred–pound doors inoperative. The blast and heat also ignited the ammunition inside the vehicle, and it was beginning to cook-off. A cook-off is what happens when the heat from the fire inside the vehicle is so intense that it causes the ammunition boxes inside the vehicle to explode. In a cook-off situation, with several thousand rounds carried inside the vehicle, you have to get out of that vehicle—quickly!

Amazingly, three of the four soldiers were able to exit the vehicle by shedding their body armor and other items and crawling out the hole from the explosion! Captain Black observed the truck commander pull himself out of the burning, gapping hole. The commander moved quickly, as if he had practiced this a thousand times over. The gunner and driver of the truck that was struck pulled themselves out through the gunner's hole on the top of the vehicle while flames were rolling over the backside.

Things took an awful turn at this point. Captain Black looked at the truck commander and saw that he had a horrific expression on his face. It was that moment of realization when he knew that one of the soldiers was trapped and possibly burning to death. Captain Black felt his stomach turn. The fourth soldier was injured in the vehicle and could not escape.

Once they realized this, the soldiers went with him back to the truck. The noncommissioned offer, the truck commander, proceeded to try to extract the trapped soldier, who had a broken arm from the impact of the blast and was unable to stand and climb out of the explosion hole. The flames burned the commander's head and neck. At this point came the loud pops of fifty caliber rounds and 7.62mm rounds as they were "cooking off" and were now exploding from the fierce fire erupting from the truck. The truck commander ran toward the oncoming chaos of armor-penetrating rounds and blazing fire. He grasped the door handle of the dismount's door and attempted to pry the door open. This went on for about ten seconds, without getting the door open.

Then the commander instructed the soldier in the truck to take off his protective gear and try to exit through the breach. The injured soldier was still confused from being knocked unconscious, with shrapnel to his head, severe hearing loss, and blurry vision, which prevented him from escaping the truck on his own. With the flames and bursting ammo intensifying with every passing second, the noncommissioned officer called his driver forward to assist in pulling their crewmember to safety. With intense physical effort, the two of them succeeded.

At this point, Captain Black had a sinking feeling that his dream, or his nightmare, had just come true. The truck went into recovery action drills, and Captain Black had a front seat view of a vehicle in front of his burning inside a mountain of soda bottles. The patrol was in the soda bottle district of the market, which has twelve-foot-high stacks of two-liter soda bottles lining the streets.

These soldiers knew their standard operating procedures, and that is why they are alive today. They appeared to be moving instinctively. The gunner and driver quickly made their way to a safe location from the truck and took cover. This is an excerpt of the write-up from the Silver Star recommendation for the commander:

"His crew received a direct hit to the left side of their truck by a single explosive formed projectile … With the flames and bursting ammo intensifying with every passing second … with intense physical effort … [pulled] their crew member to safety all the while taking further injuries … [he] sustained burns to the left side of his head and neck in addition to the 5 pieces of shrapnel in his shoulder from the IED blast … [his] blatant act of heroism and gallantry in the face of fire while injured saved the lives of three crewmembers."

Would you—better yet, could you—physically go into a large, burning armored vehicle with the knowledge that you will be burned or possibly even die? Most people can't truthfully say that they could do this, but soldiers take care of each other. That is the bottom line. It is a good feeling to have that trust and camaraderie.

After the attack, the nearby mosque was blasting out Arabic voices almost as if they were a cheering section to the horrific attack. The mosque was right across the street, and the truck they were chasing all along was sitting there, a witness to the whole event.

While the NP were securing the area, Captain Black sent in an additional patrol that came to support the search of the mosque. The attack appeared to have been coordinated with the permission of the mosque. The bomb was practically on their front doorstep. The battalion commander for the NP arrived. As the commander approached, Captain Black told him that he wanted to speak to the Imam of that mosque. After many failed attempts of getting the Imam out, the commander went in himself with his men.

Later, I would find out that this was a bad move for the NP's relationship with the Jeesh al-Mahdi militia in the area. The local militia is used to running the show around here, and the Americans and Iraqi armed forces had largely left them alone in the past. The Jeesh al-Mahdi largely controlled most of Sadr City, but they did not want incidents like this in the immediate neighborhoods. They live here.

Later that day, the Iraqi battalion commander met with our team chief at the NP operating base (our combat outpost) for the first time. The operating base had not seen mortar attacks in about six months. It was a place of income for most of the locals who worked on the construction of the post; they would not want to bomb themselves. The construction company knew that many of the locals were Jeesh al-Mahdi, but they were the only labor available. As we finished our recovery operations, an hour later across the city at our combat outpost (Hope) we would receive a barrage of mortars that would send a definite message to my team and the NP. The Iraqi battalion commander had just come from the incident with Captain Black to the meeting with the team chief. The Iraqi commander couldn't remember Captain Black's name and referred to him as Naqeeb (captain). From then on was born the nickname Geeb, short for Naqeeb. Captain Black had been a part of a large incident in Sadr City and our combat outpost, and we always joked that he had caused an international incident. He will forever be known as the "Geeb."

The soldiers involved in the incident were all returned to their base and eventually were evacuated by military helicopter to the large hospital in the Green Zone of Baghdad. They all sustained shrapnel wounds, serious burns, busted eardrums, and broken limbs. But they are alive, and being alive is a gift, one that we sometimes take for granted. Of course there is more to life than simply being alive; there is the act of living. How you see the world affects how you live in that world. It is your perspective, and never have I seen such a mix of perspectives as I did in this tour in Iraq. §

12

Perspective

"These rose colored glasses that I'm lookin' through see only beauty 'cause they hide all the truth."—John Conlee, "Rose Colored Glasses"

MONTH SIX

I was feeling bad about having to be over in Iraq for one year. I missed my family and was getting secondhand news about my children growing up. It was extremely depressing. Whenever I got like this, I would go down to the little coffee shop and then go visit the little store on the small operating base. The team was at the combat outpost, and I was only on the base when coordinating supplies and support for the team. These conversations all happened on the same day as I proceeded around the base to coordinate support.

I went in to the little coffee shop on the forward operating base and struck up a conversation with the guys who worked there.

They were from Pakistan and were very friendly. I asked one of them how long he had been in Iraq and was expecting him to say something like six months or so. "Five and a half years," was the answer I got! Wow! He had almost been here the entire time since the beginning of Operation Iraqi Freedom. In that time, I had been back and forth to Iraq and Kuwait twice. I had been promoted and worked three different jobs and had been to two army schools. My children had grown up, and I had spent many happy times with them.

To me it would be unbelievable to be away from my family for so long. How many soccer games, how many Boy Scouts meetings, how many times had I gone to church with my family in that time? If I could count them up, remember each time, and play them all back in my head at this moment. I would.

I continued my conversation with the Pakistani guys (anything to get my mind off where I was). The coffee guy said that he had worked at the PX and at the coffee shop for the entire five and a half years. He and his coffee shop friends were from Pakistan. They spoke good English and decent Arabic. They were not soldiers of course, but they had been living around us and working around us the entire time. The man I talked with told me that he sent all his money home, and that his family lived frugally off the small wages he made from the coffee shop. The Pakistani guys were allowed to eat in the mess hall and live in similar surroundings to the soldiers, which allowed him to save even more of his money for his family.

His perspective: He sees Iraq as a positive opportunity to provide for his family in Pakistan, with a good income that they would normally not be able to get. We don't usually think about it this way. How could anyone look at a war as an opportunity? I realized how my own perspective affected how I lived and acted. What I believe is not what the Pakistanis I met believed. With a relatively good lifestyle, plenty of money, and a great family, I could not fathom the thought that someone could actually enjoy his or her lot in life of being stuck in Iraq. Surely no man could enjoy being in Iraq. But here he was. Here was the one guy I thought I would not run into. This man was happy. He was making more for his family than he could ever make in his home country.

I left the coffee shop in a state of amazement. My head was spinning and I could barely comprehend the conversation I had just had. I continued to another part of the base to conduct my errands. I went to get on the Internet and the phone to coordinate with contracting. In a conversation I had with someone in contracting on Camp Victory, they were complaining about all the hours that they had to work answering e-mails and said that they would no longer accept e-mails. They wanted everyone to come in to process paperwork in person. This is a ridiculous request, given the fact that we have e-mail, scanners, and fax machines. You have to drive out on a combat mission across several miles of risky combat areas to arrive at the base. It would take an entire convoy to move to this area and that would take several days. I reminded this person that I would gladly trade being shot at, mortared, and rocketed for the rough job they had dealing with the e-mail. They had the opportunities to go to nice places and relax whenever they wanted. They had plenty of people in their organization to cover down for them. On a transition team we barely have enough people to send one person away on leave and still function. They could have it much worse.

I went to the motor pool to check on some maintenance issues and had another conversation when I happened upon a military mechanic (staff sergeant), a Kellogg, Brown and Root (KBR) contractor, and another contractor, who were all discussing how bad they had it, being stationed on the remote operating base they were on.

They were talking about how being stationed on this operating base was considered to be punishment. The staff sergeant said that it was where they sent all the people in his unit who had screwed up, and it was the worst place you could be. The KBR guy agreed and said the same thing. They also talked about their plans to try and get themselves and their soldiers to a place called "Freedoms Rest" (an old palace with a nice pool where soldiers can go for a four-day pass), and they wanted to go to Qatar on a four-day pass.

I interjected this thought into the conversation—my team and I are stationed on a remote outpost named Hope. You are stationed here, with a PX (small store), a chow hall, a gym, a mayor cell, Internet access, and an MWR (phones, internet, and movies). We don't have any of that. When we come to this operating base that you are standing on, it is considered to be our rest and relaxation. We are told we will never see "Freedoms Rest" or Qatar while we are here. Neither of you ever leave the operating base. We leave the wire and go on missions constantly. Perspective, I thought to myself.

Later in the day I ran into one of the explosive ordnance disposal soldiers. who said to me that he really appreciated having us at our outpost (Hope). The changes that we had made, the way we treated them, and the little gym equipment we bought out of our own pockets and took with us to the outpost made it a nice place for them when they weren't on the road. They considered Hope to be their rest and relaxation!

The best perspective story is the last one. A woman named Denise was in the United States, and she was a friend of one of our team members. She was writing to the team about things we needed mailed to us from the states. She wanted to help us with kitchen items such as hot plates, dishes, silverware, and bowls. She purchased several hundred dollars worth of cooking equipment and got the correct 220-volt items for Iraq. Denise had terminal cancer and had little more than months to live. Her dying wish was not to reflect on her life and worry about meeting her maker, as I am sure most of us would do. Her dying wish was to see that we had everything we needed and to make our lives a little better.

Perspective: Somebody always has it worse than you do. It isn't always that easy to see because of how difficult things may seem to you. It is your own ideas that make things seem difficult or not so difficult to bear.

It just depends on how you see the world. §

13

The Choppers

> "I hear the choppers comin', they're flyin' overhead"—old U.S. Army cadence

MONTH SEVEN

The choppers are coming. Just like the cadence says. When I heard the helicopters coming in, I wondered how many times before that soldiers had done this. Probably everything I have ever done in the army has been done before. The old-timers tell you this. but when you are young you think you know everything, and you don't listen to them. I'm not so young anymore. My hair is beginning to turn gray. As the years pass, you begin to realize more and more how much it is that you don't know. You only know your little piece of the puzzle. You really begin to see it as you get more senior in rank and years in the army.

"They're flyin' overhead," I hummed to myself. The re-supply "birds" were now our lifeline. It is pitch black outside as they arrive.

The team and some other soldiers are all standing outside near the helipad waiting on them to drop supplies to us in a sling load operation. When the choppers arrive, it is a horrendous experience because of the rotor wash and the fine sand that goes *everywhere*! We wait with several trucks nearby to quickly grab all of the supplies and equipment and get it off the helipad. The choppers bring us food, water, mail, supplies, ammo, and people. You never know who is going to get off of those choppers. Sometimes it is a private and sometimes it is a general. In the past we would get supplies from a supply convoy; however, the route clearance vehicles that go out looking for mines have all been blown up. These are the "clearance teams" that go out and clear the route so the convoy can drive behind them (and still get blown up). These guys are the only reason that we can drive down the route to our supply base. Now we can't leave at all.

The choppers bring everything. Rumor has it that two birds have been shot down recently. So they are scrutinizing requests for air travel because of this. Without them, we would be in trouble. Several times we have been told by our guys who work at the joint security station that the supplies and food run out. This could easily happen to us. No one seems too concerned about it. Why should they worry? They don't coordinate the food and supplies (but I do).

The logistics officer of our partner coalition unit that provides us with supplies is working his tail off. The only option for him to push supplies is to do it on a black status route. Black means that it is essentially completely off-limits to movement of U.S. forces without having several things. These are tanks, helicopters, extra security forces, and a route clearance team to clear the route of mines and IEDs. How would you like to go out on patrol every single day knowing you are going to get hit? That is what these guys do for a living.

The route clearance guys stay with us in our building every couple of days when they are passing through, so we try to take care of them as much as we can. Somebody should give these guys an award or something.

They are always moving and always getting blown up. We see them at different locations while everyone is on the battlefield … our friends … the ones who take care of us and we take care of them. The explosive ordnance guys, the aircraft controllers, the route clearance teams, the transition teams, the quick reaction forces, we all know each other. You have to.

The saying goes that a month in Iraq is like a lifetime. Another one says that if you don't like the current situation, just wait a month and it will change, and wait another month and it will change back. In one month, we had moved to a different operating base, changed out our brigade level team, changed out our sister battalion's team, changed out our security augments, changed coalition force partner unit, and changed out our vehicles for another type. It was a great deal of change.

The route we drove was still a black status level. People were still being killed. We were warned to be extra careful during General Petraeus's address to Congress on 9/11. JAM was looking to kidnap a transition team again. They were actively targeting people in our area. I was glad I was not the only one who was getting older. General Petraeus looked older and tired. He was briefing Congress in a different time zone, so he should have been sleeping. Congress was riding him hard. He was well prepared with his data, but he did not come across well with some of the arguments that were thrown his way.

Almost a month later, I realized that I was on the other end of this scenario. Ramadan was now winding down. My job up until that point had primarily relied on providing funding to solve our issues and various issues with the NP. I had about ten times the amount of money for the Iraqis as I did for us. But we did okay. After I left to go down and clear out all of the funds, I got stuck at the operating base for various supply reasons and was unable to return to Hope.

Now I was on the other end and would have to push supplies to my folks out at Hope. They were running out of food, water, supplies. I knew this time would come. Logisticians predict this kind of stuff. Predicting is hard to do when the plan is always changing, though. The building had to have some major renovations done to it for various reasons, necessitating turning off the water and power to the building at various times. Basically the whole situation sucked. Suck it up, cupcake.

We assembled ammunition, supplies, food, water, and mail and coordinated with the Brigade Support Battalion to conduct a night sling load mission. We were told that it was easier to get support for NPTT and MITT teams than it was for regular units. We had priority for support at the time. We got lucky.

Luck is part of transition team life. So is begging for supplies and food. So is busting your hump. For what? Now that I was seven months into this tour, I realized how many times a day we asked ourselves that question. (Stay fluid because flexible is too rigid.)

A great deal of my life in Iraq was spent on helicopter rides going to various bases to coordinate support for the team. Many times I would have to hop from one flight to another and catch a connecting flight. This required you to travel light, which for me was more than 80 pounds of protective gear, ammo, and my helmet. In addition, I usually had to take my laptop and my carryon bag and two weapons. Altogether, this was probably about 150 pounds of weight besides my body. Protocol for our team was to always go out and meet our team members when they came back from a mission like this. Usually the team guy had been doing this type of travel for a week or more, so being helped with your bags and equipment from the chopper to your room was a great way to be welcomed home to the outpost.

On one particular mission I had several adventures. I had made my way out to the helipad at the outpost. It was pitch black outside. By the time you walk the couple of hundred feet out to the helipad, you have a nice little bead of sweat on you going from the top of your head to the soles of your feet. All of the 150 pounds you take with you is on your back, and you are humping it through fine, beach-like sand. I hadn't even made it on the chopper yet when I heard a rapid "crack, crack, crack." It was the sound of not-so-distant AK-47 rifle fire. This was a sound that I had been forced to get used to. The Iraqi security personnel were shooting at something outside the outpost perimeter. During our tour in Iraq, we heard that sound more days than not. I looked up and could see the perimeter tower, and I could tell the guard was firing. I stood and talked to the inner security guard (a U.S. soldier) as I waited for the choppers.

The choppers arrived in a rhythmic hail of whooshing and whooping air, chopped by the massive blades as the helicopters blasted sand and rocks and whatever else around hundreds of feet in the air. Normally, you would want to walk away and avoid being by something creating this much havoc, but you have to force yourself to go forward and approach it. This is your ride out of the hellhole outpost.

I jumped on. I was lucky this time and had a seat in the middle section facing forward. I was able to see out the front windows of the helicopter. It is quite a thrill to watch out those windows as you travel throughout Iraq. It was sunset when we departed and a dark night sky by the time we arrived at our destination. It is a powerful feeling to be loaded down with all that firepower and ability to maneuver in the air on that helicopter.

As I flew over the *mulhallas* of Baghdad, I watched the barefoot children playing soccer, I saw explosions, and I heard rounds fired as we continued our journey. I had the eerie dream feeling coming over me, and it was as if the neighborhoods themselves were trying to talk to me in this dream. They were saying, "Go home." The helicopter fired off some chafe (like fireworks), and this woke me up out of my daydream.

I was prepared as always to live and work for several weeks on my own at the supply base, gathering and coordinating for the team's support. Food, water, ammunition, basic household supplies, some supplies for the Iraqis, and whatever I could get for individual team members that they had requested was on the agenda. The gathering began almost the instant I got off the helicopter. Before I even went to drop my equipment in my room, I would touch base with a few of my contacts to make sure they had not returned to the states. Many times I would barter some items I had that my contacts had not had good luck in obtaining, like some wood or other supplies. The front lines of Iraq was a difficult place to obtain supplies, so you had to be creative.

It was always hot, and the majority of soldiers on the supply base were allowed to walk around in their physical training uniform with a weapon. When I was gathering supplies and equipment, I wore this uniform. Many of my contacts were enlisted soldiers, and it was a little less intimidating I thought, because I was a captain. It was also a little weird to be a captain and doing so much labor to load trucks and supplies and things, and it was a lot easier to get some help loading if they thought I was just a soldier on a loading detail. It worked pretty well most of the time.

The supply base was big, and it was a constant target for insurgents. It was pretty well protected from the attacks that happened every few days, but sometimes the attacks were bad, mostly rocket and mortar attacks and a few snipers. Life just went on ten minutes or so after the attack, when you went back to what you were doing ... most of the time. You still had to be careful, but it was a little more laid back than being at the outpost.

It took a few days to lay on transportation for the supplies and to gather them up. I obtained an extra twenty-foot shipping container to use to consolidate my supplies. Then I would get guidance on how the next supply mission would happen. At the time it was going to be a sling load mission, in which the helicopters drop in the supplies. This required an extra step in my duties. I would have to take all the supplies and equipment to a central yard and put them on special pallets with nets and slings so they could be lifted and dropped into our outpost by the helicopters.

Most of the time my teammates would say I was on vacation and would make fun of me, but they didn't realize that I worked more when I was on this so-called vacation than I did on the outpost. It was especially difficult to do this by myself. Occasionally, a few folks would come down to help me out but not always. On some occasions, I became a de facto rear detachment. I would receive whoever was coming down from the outpost and get them set up and ready to do whatever business that they had to do. It was just easier to leave me in place many times at the supply base for whatever reason.

I organized and finished my business on the supply mission and prepared for the sling load mission the next evening. The rocket and mortar attacks were pretty bad on this particular trip. I remember this distinctly because I was asleep in a large building when I was shaken awake by an explosion that caused dust and debris to fly everywhere. My room was protected with wood and Kevlar panels, but I would not have survived a direct hit to my room (later in my tour, my room was hit by a rocket). It was this thought that made me into a light sleeper. I could jump out of a sound sleep and roll onto the floor in a matter of seconds. Now I did roll onto the floor and crept out in the hallway to wait with all the other personnel. We were sitting in the hallway on the floor where the protection of the building would shield us best from a direct impact.

These were weird moments in the middle of the night when you really got to know your neighbors who slept in the various rooms in the building. This happened many, many, many times. The rockets began and did not end for several hours. Eventually the explosions stopped, and we heard the all-clear signal come over the intercom. I got about an hour of sleep and then woke up to prepare for a long day of coordinating and consolidating supplies for a sling load mission.

In the morning I ensured that the supplies were consolidated and met with the sergeant in charge of the mission. Later in the afternoon I assisted with rigging and creating the eight or so pallets that would go on the sling load mission. This took a good portion of the day, and when we were done we loaded them on a truck to go out to the helipad, and then we went and grabbed some dinner. We would be up late that night waiting on the helicopters to arrive and connect the loads and then deliver them. The helicopters took turns of about three trips to deliver all the loads. I waited on the helipad with all my equipment as the helicopters left to deliver the cargo and then returned for another load. I would ride back with the final mission and return to Hope.

We conducted the sling load operation and it was a success. It really helped morale for those guys who were at Hope to know that someone on the other end cared about them. I will never forget the sound of the choppers—the sound of Hope. §

Photo Section

Figure 1. Trash is everywhere in Iraq with smoke and sand. This view is a typical patrol driving the streets of Sadr City.

Figure 2. This is the combat action badge. It provides special recognition to soldiers who personally engage or are engaged by the enemy during combat operations.

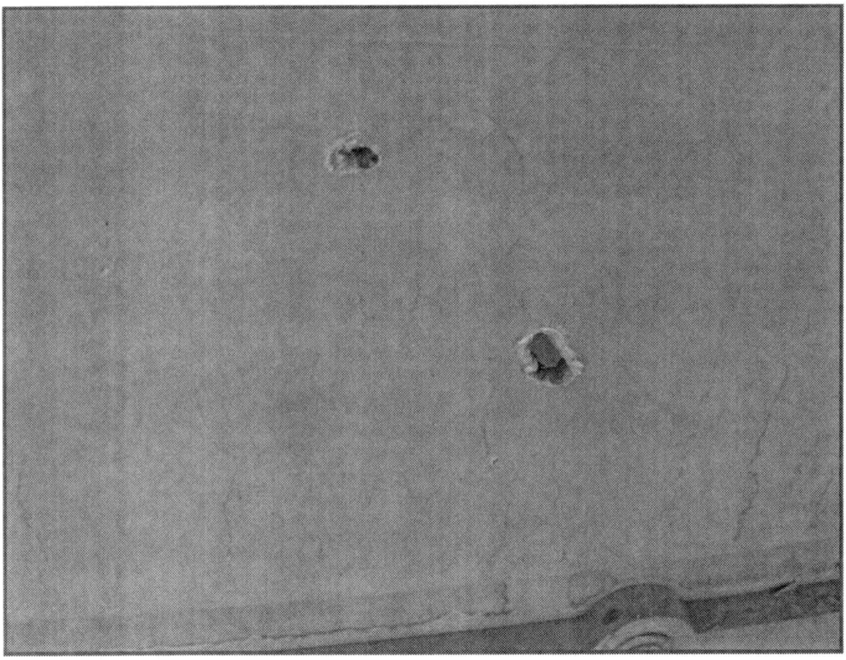

Figure 3. The first damage to our Humvee in combat. Several small holes are visible in the extremely thick armor plating on the vehicle.

Figure 4. Stryker vehicle at a security station is about to go out on a night patrol.

Figure 5. Sadr City as viewed from above during a mission that required us to move by helicopter across Baghdad.

Figure 6. Iraqi cultural training at Fort Riley. We wore the clothes, ate the food, and drank chai with Iraqi actors to get a feel for the culture.

Figure 7. Our living area at Fort Riley was tight. When we put on all our gear and got ready to move to training, it was packed.

Figure 8. The rifle range, minus the snow.

Figure 9. This image in the back ground of this artist rendering of Dante's Inferno is what came to mind at the first Combat Outpost.

Figure 10. Not the actual building but this bombed out building looks very similar to what the first outpost actually looked like.

Figure 11. A view from inside the first outpost that we encountered during our tour in Iraq.

Figure 12. A vehicle being recovered after a large blast.

Figure 13. Conducting preparations and inspections prior to going out on a patrol. We were involved in a long firefight that night.

Figure 14. Conducting a joint mission with the national police in Sadr Crity Iraq.

Figure 15. Backseat view in a Humvee driving through Baghdad on a mission. Someone fired shots at the rear of our convoy on this day.

Figure 16. A view of our trail chopper as we depart our logistics base for the combat outpost.

Figure 17. A great view from inside the helicopter as we fly over Baghdad on a mission.

Figure 18. The sign at the front of our combat outpost.

14

Rocket's Red Glare

"And the rockets' red glare … the bombs bursting in air …"—Sir Francis Scott Key, "The Star Spangled Banner"

MONTH SEVEN

Sssshhhhhiiiiooooooooo … Boom! That was a rocket. I was walking to get some food, and I was in the middle of a large parking lot. I watched calmly as the rocket zoomed over my head at approximately two hundred feet off the ground, seemingly in slow motion. As I continued to watch, the rocket impacted and exploded a hundred and fifty meters directly in front of me near the location I was walking to, the chow hall. I knew what to do this time. I knew the direction of travel, the type of round, the distance, and the approximate spot where the next one would land. I went the other way and ducked down low behind a military container in a parking area, down on the ground … and waited.

The second rocket fired and impacted in almost the exact same spot.

My anxiety level was high in anticipation of this tasking that I was on and the rockets weren't helping my nerves at all. I was currently visiting a small base, waiting on a ride on a combat patrol. Then I would travel on through several connections of small flights to get to different bases. The tasking was to be the battalion representative at the security station. This is a rotated duty among our team members. Working at the security station was a mixed bag, like everything else in Iraq. On the one hand, you were away from the team and all the bull for a while, and you got a lot of time to yourself. On the other hand, you were humping your full combat load around Sadr City doing various types of patrols with coalition and Iraqi forces, not a fun job.

The feeling when the rocket exploded was—relief, not what I would have expected to feel like. However, I was relieved the rocket had not hit me. I no longer had to wait and worry about when and if something was going to happen to me during this time. It had just happened. I did not want to feel that way, but I did. Now I could stop worrying about it, and if another one happened … oh well. This was too much to worry about. It was too stressful to put that kind of worry on yourself to constantly think about dying. There was so many ways to die around Iraq. If it happens, it happens (meaning, dying from something in combat). The words from an old, familiar song were playing in my head. My mind wandered as I hummed something nervously. I had a habit of humming or singing a little song to myself when I was nervous. The red glare … how did that song go? It made my mind wander back to that place of daydreams and the haze. A large cloud had formed now where the rocket had impacted. I sat and waited to hear the all-clear signal, humming to myself an old familiar song ... one that I hadn't sung in a long time.

The funny thing was that I had not even made it to the security station yet. To get to the security station I had to fly by helicopter to the small operating base where our brigade level team lived, spend the night at that operating base, and the go on a combat patrol with them through Sadr City the next morning and then finally be dropped off at the security station to relieve my NCO. I was still at the small operating base of my brigade team and had just woken up after sleeping for four and a half hours. I was walking to the meeting point where the brigade team got the vehicles and personnel together for the morning's combat patrol when the rockets hit. I was going to get some food. but I guessed I wasn't going to get any now.

A couple of hours prior I had spoken to a civilian contractor who worked on the early warning radar system for the operating base. It sets off an alarm that screams in a human voice: "Incoming! Incoming! *Beep, beep!* Incoming! Incoming! *Beep, beep!*" We traded stories about various rockets, mortars, explosions, and attacks. One thing we discussed was how people run to the bunkers around them. "Don't run, because you could run into the explosion," he said. "Get down on the ground. Because when the mortars hit, they blow up in the air." That was good advice. He also explained to me why the radar does not always catch all the incoming mortars and rockets.

My NCO had been at the security station for almost two weeks. Our team chief had promised not to leave him there that long, but he had no choice. When they dropped him off. my NCO had told the team guys that were on the convoy, "I'll see you next month." That was in September, and it was now October.

Our combat patrol was five hours long. That is a brutal amount of time to be driving around in full combat load. We were following the brigade commander of the NP around Sadr City. He was doing what NP commanders usually do—showboating. They like to go out and personally take charge of operations and actually conduct the operation themselves. It is unimaginable to think of a brigade commander in the U.S. Army doing something like this. It just would not happen.

This guy was a trip. He was walking around neighborhoods with his son dressed just as he was in green army fatigues. An entourage of NP security personnel, U.S. Army advisors, and U.S. Army security personnel followed as he wandered around. He was knocking on doors or screaming at vendors on the street who were violating parking codes. His approach, seemingly to the American mind to be without purpose, may have made some sense to the native Iraqi. He was demonstrating his *wasta* (Iraqi machismo) with the fact that he was willing to walk around with his son in tow, without a flak vest or helmet (we all had them on, inside the vehicles). I would never risk my son's life to do something like that, but I am not Iraqi.

Wasta is an important concept in this culture. It is about position, power, and the attitude that one has more than others do. That is why the Iraqi military hoards supplies and equipment. They were poor and mistreated under Saddam Hussein. Perhaps they do not yet fully understand the opportunities that exist in the new world that was created for them. Maybe they do understand it better than we think they do. Maybe they are preparing for what they believe to be the inevitable end to all of this. This is an end that Americans will not shape or determine for them.

These things are all intermingled together with the stress, the incompetence, the desperateness of the situation, and the lack of sleep. I tried to distract myself away from it with work, exercise, or writing this book. I felt a little better when I talked to my family on the phone, but at the same time it made me think about the things that I did not want to think about, like the fact that not only was I risking my life (that is a given) but I was also risking my family's future. A future without a father is not fair to a child. They need parents to help them survive, grow, and develop. How would my children remember me? Someone who fought … for what? For something, I believed in? For my team? For the good ol' U.S. of A.? What is an adequate epitaph for my tombstone? I can't think of one that sounds good.

War on terror, insurgents, our national security—that stuff doesn't matter when the rockets fly, when the bombs burst, and when the rounds whiz past you. It is hard to live day to day in this manner. Some days it is unbearable, knowing that it goes on and on for so many years.

A soldier's hope is that he fights when told to do so, accomplishes the mission in the best manner possible, and then comes home. This war has been fought by relatively the same people on their third, fourth, and some even on their fifth involuntary tours in Iraq. That is an incredible burden for so few Americans to carry.

Hope is an ironic name for a place in Iraq. It is also what Francis Scott Key was trying to tell us about when he wrote the phrase "proof through the night" in his poem in 1814, as he watched the flag raise defiantly over Fort McHenry as the British continuously bombarded the fort with shells. The flag was the proof and the hope. I think about things like this when I look at how others in history have made it through hard times. I have tried to be positive and keep my cup half-full, but it is hard.

The words of that old familiar song went through my mind repeatedly on that day as I hummed nervously, the song that I had sung so many times as a young boy in school, the song that means so much to Americans. It inspires hope in us and our future even under the direst of circumstances. It inspired hope in me that day, like those who were inspired by the sight of that tattered flag raised in defiance toward an enemy.

I figured out what song it was and why it had come to my mind. For you see, like the song, there was a red glare that day from the rockets.

"And the rocket's red glare, the bombs bursting in air, gave proof through the night that our flag was still there." §

15

Flashback

"What's in a name? That which we call a rose by any other name would smell as sweet."—William Shakespeare, *Romeo and Juliet*

APRIL 2004—BLACK SUNDAY

The smell is anything but sweet. It is the most awful smell you could ever encounter. Decades of raw sewage in the middle of the street smells really bad. The baking sun accentuates the stench. The smell is coming from the market area in Sadr City. You can smell it all the way to our outpost, several miles away—Combat Outpost Hope. This is the American name. The Iraqi name is *al-amal*. It was not always called Hope by the Americans. Many times I'd wondered, "Why Hope?" It was so obvious that I could not see it. Hope, Prosperity, Loyalty, Victory—these were all outpost names involving good things, positive things. It was a move by our forces to get away from the aggressive military names used by army units.

Typically an army unit will name its area either after a soldier who died in combat or maybe their unit motto.

A few years ago Hope was called Combat Outpost War Eagle. This is after the War Eagles of the Second Armored Cavalry Regiment. The outpost was a grisly scene several years ago, where eight soldiers were killed and more than sixty were wounded in an intense battle on April 4, 2004. This was Palm Sunday, now referred to by family members and soldiers of the unit as Black Sunday. Little did we know that several soldiers had died here in 2004, a couple of meters from where we slept at night. Also, the medical station where more than sixty people were treated for gunshot wounds was about twenty feet from us. Several hundred armed soldiers faced more than five thousand militia members of the Jeesh al-Mahdi forces here. It is considered by many to be the beginning of the insurgency in Iraq. The battle has had lasting effects on how we handle the war in Iraq and specifically in Sadr City, like the fact that no one goes into the northern part of Sadr City to this day because of that involvement. There is a definitive line of demarcation along one route in Sadr City that effectively cuts the city in half. and it is a well known fact that U.S. forces do not go past it. This engagement also resulted in the rule that no more unarmored Humvees were to be outside of operating bases.

In the war up until this time, the Americans had paid little mind to militants in Sadr City because they were overstretched and had their attention on other areas. It seems we had a limited insight into the local population and a lack of understanding about what was brewing in Sadr City at the time—an insurgency. The major population in Sadr City at the time was angered at the fact that Paul Bremer, the U.S. administrator in Iraq, had ordered the closure of the *Al-Hawza* newspaper because of its anti-American rhetoric. This fervor and the incident that followed caused an uprising of the city.

It was the last patrol of the day. The convoy was on a peacekeeping mission escorting a (pardon the graphic language) shit-sucking truck. The United States was paying to have contractors go into the heart of Sadr City slums to suck out decades worth of raw liquid sewage that filled the streets. This was in a move to try and win over the locals and assist with public service projects.

The 2-2 Armored Cavalry Regiment (ACR) was the unit originally responsible for the area, but they had to leave a month prior to the arrival of the new units. The 1-2 ACR was chosen to come in, fill the gap, and take over for a month while the 2-5 ACR arrived and took control of the area. Many of the tanks and other equipment that the unit would normally have brought with them to Iraq was left in the states. The unit was told that they were going to embark on more of a humanitarian mission, so the equipment would not be needed.

The patrol of soldiers that were tasked to escort the sewage trucks were on the way back to Combat Outpost War Eagle (now Hope). Lieutenant Abraham was in charge of the patrol. As the patrol passed a mosque, one of the soldiers noticed a militiaman dressed in black. At the time, we had no clue how organized or how big the Mahdi army had become. The weapon was confiscated, everything searched, and eventually it was returned. The incident created a ruckus that sparked a massive angry mob in the city streets. The residents of this city were coming together as an armed force to take out some anger on the U.S. soldiers. The streets were blocked with concrete and burning trash and tires, channeling the convoy into areas where the militia was prepared to attack them from every rooftop and street.

I spoke to one of the noncommissioned officers working at the security station that day. He was here for his third Iraq tour and was in the battle in 2004. He said that they were given bad intelligence and the updates were not passed along properly to their unit. The soldiers that went out on the patrol that day had no idea that the entire city wanted to kill them!

The convoy was attacked by thousands of Mahdi militia. Estimates state that five thousand Mahdi militiamen were faced by several hundred soldiers. The Mahdi used women and children in the front ranks and sent waves of people into the streets to surround the convoy. The convoy was eventually pinned down and, after a number of failed rescue attempts, finally succeeded in getting back to Hope.

The fighting continued even after this incident, with the Mahdi seizing control of government and municipal buildings and numerous police stations in Sadr City. Battles ensued throughout the city with the Mahdi.

U.S. forces had to take tanks and helicopters in to gain control of the police stations and government buildings. At the time it was viewed as a major turning point, from what was supposed to be a peacekeeping mission to a full-fledged fight against an insurgency.

In 2006, a ceremony was conducted where the local unit commander for the U.S. Army handed control of the installation over to the Iraqi Army. This is the first occurrence of the name Hope that I was able to find on the Internet and in the media. We are told that shortly thereafter the Iraqi Army abandoned Hope.

Abandon Hope to return again one day soon. We are told that the Iraqi Army will once again come to this place. How many more times will we come back to this place? Maybe they should change the name to Progress.

One final note: this particular battle involved Cindy Sheehan's son. Cindy Sheehan is a very vocal antiwar and anti-Bush critic. She lives near former President Bush's property in Texas and has frequently been seen on the news demonstrating against the war. Her son was killed during the battle that day. §

16

The Raid

"There are only two types of soldiers that you need to worry about, the quick and the dead. Which one are you private?"—My basic training drill sergeant

SOMEWHERE IN SADR CITY, 3:00 am, ON PATROL WITH U.S. ARMY AND THE IRAQI NATIONAL POLICE

Screaming as loud as I could, I replied to my drill sergeant's question, *"The quick, Drill Sergeant!"* Eighteen years later, it was the thought in my head that makes me move along a dark street in Sadr City in the middle of the night.

Communications and radio equipment were always my weak area in training at Fort Riley, but not today. I had asked the commo guy (the radio specialist) several times about the settings on my radio. I was trying to get my antiquated radio to work. It was a great radio but could not compare with the advanced equipment being used by the infantry guys. They joked with me that I should probably get another radio. The commo guy sat with me on my third attempt and watched me as I loaded my own radio and proceeded to show him its clock. "I'm impressed, sir," said the young army specialist (E4). He continued, "Most people can't even get to that point with the radio settings." The commo guy realized then that I had set up the radio correctly and that he had given me the wrong settings. I threw back my own comment at this point, "Guess it wasn't my radio after all, huh, specialist?"

I continued to conduct my own personal pre-combat checks on my equipment immediately after being briefed about the upcoming mission for the night. I would be a ride-along, one of the various special guys that a combat unit has to baby-sit when they go out on a mission. At this point, I had been in a few firefights and one other raid.

"I need more ammunition," I thought to myself. I already had a black bag, my "go bag," full of extra ammunition, batteries, some food, and water. As a visitor, you never want to assume the people you are with operate the way you do. Everybody does things a little differently. I found another hundred rounds of ammo and threw it all in my bag. Most of my movements around Iraq lately were by helicopter, so I had to really scrutinize the load I was carrying. Ammo was heavy, but you can never have enough of it.

After checking my equipment, and testing everything, I did a gut check and realized I really was not nervous about the mission. We were a heavily armed force with a decent plan. It was that strange feeling of security in a situation that would have caused most people to freak out. Everyone was comfortable with each other; they knew each other, the NP, the infantry guys, and the interpreters.

I walked down the stairs from the security station to go out to the vehicle, and my foot slipped. *Blood*, I thought. I caught myself and looked down. The step was marble and it was just slick, but no blood. Twice in previous months, I had climbed these steps and had stepped in the blood of soldiers that I knew. The steps were slick, but the blood made them slicker. I pushed aside the thoughts of the mortar attacks and scenes that I had witnessed in this place, and I turned off my emotions. I did not need them right now.

After some pre-combat checks in the vehicle, we departed in our convoy formation. I was in the vehicle with the overall ground commander, an infantry captain. He wanted me around, and I liked being in that vehicle because I could hear all the radio traffic on the different nets among the battalion, the security station, and our convoy.

The raid was well planned and fairly well executed. Communication problems with the Iraqis did hamper the efforts a little bit, but things still went pretty well. What I didn't realize was that these guys had obviously been working together frequently.

After our movement to the objective, the various dismounted personnel from the vehicles secured their assigned areas. The gunners rotated to the outside of the secured area to provide security from the building rooftops to cordon off the area. I was listening to the radio, watching the security guys move, and pulling security. The infantry captain looked back at me and said, "Hey, your guys are at the door—you need to go meet your terp [interpreter]." Roger that. I announced that I was dismounting the vehicle and ran to the front of the building where the breaching element was tearing open the door. Kneeling and pulling security, I watched as a heavily armored Humvee pulled a set of heavily built iron bars from off the front door of a large building that we would enter and search in a matter of seconds. The aggressiveness of a platoon of infantry guys and an equal force of NP on a nighttime raid at 3:00 am is impressive.

That was it. That was the moment. I had passed a test, and I didn't even know it. I realized it much later as I was writing these words. When I was in the advanced course, my captain buddies and I would be sitting around joking and drinking a beer. Our joking usually revolved around the various horror stories that we had been told from the initial round of guys who had done this transition team stuff. We would say stuff like, "They can make me go on the missions but they can't make me get out of the vehicle." Although our words were only joking gestures said after a beer or two, some of us were serious and some were not. Secretly in our minds, we were sizing each other up (in combat there were only two types of people: the quick and the dead). When you are in combat, in Iraq or any other country on this planet, you are a rifleman, a soldier. So the moment had come when I had to leave that vehicle, and it felt as natural as getting up in the morning.

I followed my buddy down the wall, touched him on the back, and let him know I was there. I took a knee, peered through my night sight on my weapon, and scanned the rooftops in my sector. Then I was next to move. "Moving!" I communicated who I was and what I was doing. "Grossman, moving up the staircase! Clear! Roger, clear! Moving! I thought about my training. We had extensively practiced this same sequence in battle drills during training at Fort

Riley. Now it was for real. The breach was now complete. Time to search. "Search teams!" said the sergeant. "Moving!" the rest of us responded. My role as an advisor left me without a particular assigned position. I stuck close to the command elements.

A voice chimed in across the multiple personal radios we carried, "Shots fired." A young soldier gave me a run down, "Sir, we have a report that shots were fired, and the National Police engaged two personnel who were carrying PKCs!" PKCs were a common soviet weapon used throughout Iraq by both the military and the insurgents. It was important to get people to repeat information because they are stressed and excited and their adrenaline is flowing. "Repeat, which way were they headed?" I said. The guy pointed out the direction. The interpreter spoke to the NP several times on the issue, but each time the details changed a little. Working with an interpreter to get information back and forth between the Americans and the Iraqis was hard enough. It got harder when they were excited from being shot at.

The U.S. soldiers had their areas secure and had decided to carry on despite the shots fired. In the debrief, the only mention of this was that the NP had engaged two personnel with a short burst of about four rounds and were unable to find them after that.

The mission continued on as we searched the building. The building had about five floors to it, with a roof area accessible from the fourth floor. Once we reached the roof, a sniper team was dispatched to provide security. The noncommissioned officer in charge put me with an infantry soldier and had us secure the staircase while search teams (both American and NP) were proceeding.

The building was searched based on a tip from a call-in hotline. The tip was old, and the search did not produce anything substantial. We ex-filtrated the building, and after a short huddle all elements mounted back up in the vehicles. We did our sensitive items checks and prepared to depart.

What was my value? Was it my advice? Was it my presence? My role seemed to be fulfilled. I, my team members, and other soldiers had asked this question many times before, during, and after our tour to Iraq. Is all the effort worth it? How do you measure it? Your mind goes back to this question many times because your friends and family and the American public back home want the answer. Is the situation in Iraq a self-licking ice cream cone?

The lieutenant and the sergeant from the NP only occasionally looked in my direction throughout the night. When they did, I would smile and nod my head in a reassuring manner. (I know you can do it, was my thought.) I chimed in only once or twice in the planning process and did more observing than anything else, but in the end, on the after-action review, I had numerous details and shared what I had observed. I tried to spend as much quality time joking and laughing and talking to the Iraqis as I could during the week I was assigned to this duty. It is that level of relationship that helps you get through to them, which they value highly in their culture.

Many U.S. personnel find it difficult to deal with the Iraqis because they expect things to be solved in a U.S. manner with a U.S. solution. I learned that the more personable you are with them, the more they will like you and the more they will want to work with you. They like to joke a lot, and so do I.

The role of an advisor is unpredictable. It is dangerous. You achieve more of a balance with your soldier skills than in any staff job in any regular army unit. This was the rediscovery of what I had known from two other deployments. These were the moments taught in many lessons of many wars by many a hard-ass sergeant trainer. The most basic soldier skills (how to shoot, how to move, and how to communicate) are the ones that keep you alive in combat. §

17

The Fallen

"To fallen soldiers, let us sing
Where no rockets fly or bullets wing …
Where no mothers cry and no children weep
We will stand and guard through the angels sleep
All through the ages safely keep
The mansions of the Lord."
—Randall Wallace

"Welcome back!" The team chief and Sergeant First Class Brian Gerschank met me at the landing pad on my return flight from the tasking and grabbed my gear as I walked briskly off the helipad while the choppers lifted off behind me. It was a dark night. and I had just returned from our outpost. The smell of burning trash was clogging the hazy air. I was tired, but not too tired to pass up a sandwich at the chow hall with Brian. On the way back, we noticed them: It was a sight that makes you stop in your tracks. It brings instantaneous waves of emotion and sorrow. It brings the question about whether it is all worth it back. It reminds you of what you want to forget. It is the sight of the guidons.

The guidons are unit level flags, and the guidon bearer is a soldier who stands with the guidon in front of a formation of soldiers. With the guidon was the leadership and all the companies and battalions on the base who were standing at the helipad. It only happens for one reason.

I did not realize why they did this until one day when I saw old glory draped over what was obviously the shape of a military metal casket. There were three caskets, total. As the bodies of soldiers were taken from the field hospital to the helipad they were honored by the guidons, leaders, and soldiers who line up along the street to the helipad. On this day we saw a gathering of sweaty, dirt-covered soldiers, crying in disbelief, asking the "why" questions. Why? Why my friend? Why now? Why right before we redeploy? Why are we doing this? Why did they have to die? They are obviously the platoon or squad or team members of the soldiers in those caskets. I couldn't even turn my head to look at them. It is too hard to look and see something that could so easily happen to you.

Brian told me that he had seen many memorial services when he was at Fort Riley. I asked him if they were for transition team soldiers, and he said yes. He was a replacement for our team who showed up about three months after we arrived in Iraq. As part of the surge, our team had been one of the biggest classes to process through Fort Riley. We went through before General Petraeus took over in CENTCOM. We were the other surge that you didn't hear too much about.

Brian shared this story with me about a time at Fort Riley after the team had left for Iraq and when he was still in training. Standing in the field, he had stared up at the dark clouds rolling in. He hoped in his mind that it would not rain on the formation as they stood at attention to honor his dead comrades. The rain came and so did the twenty-one gun salute. The ceremony continued, surreal, the sounds, the rain, the feelings: they all faded away until all that could be heard was the lone bugler. The lone bugler played taps hauntingly. The feeling, the dream—it was so unreal.

Brian stood in formations like these many times, twice a week during his training cycle at Fort Riley. It had become routine. The company that trains you at Fort Riley is responsible for your memorial service, should you die in combat. In some way, it sends the message to make sure you train the soldiers well. Those words I stared at in my office for many years came to mind: "Let no man's soul cry out, had I the proper training," was written on an old World War II poster. Long ago when I was a noncommissioned officer and a staff sergeant, I kept the poster to always remind me to put my best effort into training.

Brian's story continued: the chaplain had started the service, no longer reading from his notes because his service had been repeated many times. Brian recalled that most of the services seemed to be for pairs of soldiers, with two pairs of boots, two rifles with dog tags hanging from them, and two helmets. It is a very particular arrangement of items when a fallen soldier is honored. Brian recalled that at the end of the service, they approached the memorials and rendered the proper military courtesy—a slow, sharp, well-executed salute. Not the kind of salute you give every day to an officer who outranks you as he or she is walking past. This salute was different. It was the last one.

One of the memorialized soldiers was familiar to Brian—they knew each other from church. The soldier had been a family man, with five children, and was extremely active in the post's chapel. The soldier's wife later told Brian that another memorial service was held at another army post after the one at Fort Riley. This is because the families of transition teams are spread out all over the country. As if being on a transition team wasn't hard enough, add to that the fact that your family is on another post. E-mail, Web pages, and phone contact help, but it is not a substitute for the close-knit family groups that all soldiers and their families are accustomed to in regular units.

Brian remembered listening to the length of time that the fallen had served in Iraq. Two months, nine months, six months—he could not recall any kind of pattern that made sense. The majority of deaths were from IEDs and EFPs, though some were from sniper attacks. What would that woman do with five children who now had no father?

His first ceremony like this made Brian realize that this deployment was different. He was a communications NCO and had been on deployments before, but this was not the same. He was not just going to a war; he was going to "fight" in a war. The specific skills he had been trained on in the last ten years were mainly to solve specific communications problems. Not anymore—being a soldier came first.

Brian pondered this at length until he was tasked to do his first Joint Security Stations (JSS) rotation. To date, Brian has pulled the longest rotation for our team, having been on numerous patrols and missions in Sadr City. He said that he once witnessed a U.S. soldier, an infantryman, take an AK-47 round square in the middle of his chest from a sniper. The soldier came back in from the patrol and asked if someone had a medium plate that he could borrow for his vest. He was planning to leave on the next patrol. It was at this point, seeing this young, brave soldier in action that Brian could no longer worry about when, or if, his time would come. If it comes, it comes. If it doesn't, it doesn't. Be ready for both. §

18

Room with a View

"I lie down and sleep; I wake again because the Lord sustains me. I am not afraid."—Psalm 3:5–6

MONTH EIGHT

"Dude, your room is f'—d up!"

"What the heck are you talking about?" I said to Master Sergeant Calderon in the operations center. I had just come in from running around the inside of the outpost walls, and I knew that I had made my bed and that in general my room looked okay. "No, your room at Rusty was hit by a rocket last night, and it is totally screwed." As the logistics guy, my duties often entailed going down to this main base to obtain supplies, so I would stay in that room for a week to two weeks at a time. Yikes!

First, I asked how Captain Sanchez was doing. His room was right next to mine, and he was sleeping in the room last night when somewhere between eight to eleven rockets slammed into the hospital barracks building. We had him on the phone asking questions and found out that he was okay. Later we learned that the rockets had propane tanks attached to them, with all kinds of shrapnel and ball bearings. This created incredible explosions that blew massive holes in the pavement and destroyed all the windows, doors, outer walls, and buildings in the area.

Our sister team took the brunt of the attack, with several of their rooms destroyed. All day my anxiety level was up. How many times had I slept in that room, praying to God that this would not be how it would end? Lying in bed asleep, with earplugs in my ears to reduce all the noise from the building at night (A/C, people yelling, cars and trucks blaring horns, mortars, gunfire), and not hearing the final few seconds of your life as they pass by.

Anxiety was one of the reasons that I did not sleep well. I found some Kevlar blanketing a few weeks after we had moved in to these rooms and hung several double strands of it up. Many Soldiers would just use the fatalistic approach and let it ride. They figure that if you are going to buy the farm then it was your time to go anyway, and that was your karma as a soldier. But I am not a fatalist.

Apparently God had listened to me this time, in a funny way. He spared me but not my room. That is the funny part. Prayers are often answered by God in ways that we do not understand. I understand the point just fine. I am alive because I was not in the room. The rocket hit the room and it was not my time. Everything in the room can be replaced, but my life cannot be replaced. I wrote a funny e-mail to my family about this. I guess next time I should ask God to save some of the stuff in my room also.

It seems like such a simple concept. Many people over here do not get it. They take unnecessary risks every day. You see it, and you tell them. They give you their fatalistic karma crap, and then you move on. The sheer number of times that I have had this conversation with people is in the thousands by now. "We should not do it that way," I will say. It is too dangerous, doesn't make sense, risk versus reward, task and purpose, and so on.

A few days later, I was talking to the security guys who said that Apache helicopters were already in the air around the base when the guy fired the rockets that exploded into my room. The rockets were fired at almost a ninety-degree angle early in the morning in a similar fashion to the low-flying rockets that I witnessed previously. These guys were adapting to us almost on a daily basis, watching our defenses and measuring things to know and understand how to get to us.

The rockets had been fired from a large truck moving very close to the base. Within minutes the attack helicopters came after the truck. We often joke about the amount of opium that the insurgents must smoke before they do such attacks that will almost certainly result in their deaths. Maybe they just really don't know that they will never be coming back. The joke was that this guy must have taken one big bong hit of some opium as he watched a couple of hellfire missiles coming toward his truck. Or maybe he just didn't know that he had signed his own death warrant by firing those missiles.

I had witnessed the destruction that comes from a hellfire missile in Desert Storm. The missile is attracted to the heat from the engine of the vehicle. The missile somehow burns so hot that it melts the people in the vehicle into the dash and metal frame of the vehicle. In Desert Storm, I had once seen an Iraqi soldier melted into the steering column of his vehicle. It is a ghost that haunts me to this day. I was only nineteen or twenty years old, and I have seen that sight in my mind ever since, over all these years.

This was the fate of the man who could have been the end of me had I been present in the room that day. He ended up having a much worse day than I. Was this worth giving his life? I doubt it. The truck was attacked immediately following his firing off the rockets. More than one helicopter launched their hellfire missiles at the truck. Simultaneous explosions consumed the frame and reduced it into a pile of nothing in a crater near the perimeter of the base.

It is ironic that the man who fired the missiles was reduced to a smoking pile of ashes and nothingness also by missiles.

A month or so later, I was in my room (after some extensive repairs) when another instance occurred. One of the things that immediately strikes you as the night's darkness approaches in Iraq is the smell. Not the smell of trash or stench, but the smell of burning. The trash is burned at night, and it is sometimes so thick that you can barely see a few feet in front of you. Scent is one of the strongest reminders of memories of sensations that you can have. The smell of burning leaves reminds me of very happy experiences as a child. I can recall the first moment that I smelled it, first as an eight-year-old child at the lake house of my parents. It was nothing more than a trailer on a lake, an hour and half drive away from our suburban home. The trailer had power and water, but that was it, no trash pickup and no other services. It was nestled deep in the country on a lakeshore, and that was the way we liked it.

Being from the city, as a kid I was used to everything being done for us. Getting rid of our trash at home meant taking the trash to the curb for the garbage man to pick up. At the lake, we had a burn barrel in which we had to burn our trash. I would chase the small gecko lizards around the grass around the property while the trash was burning in the burn barrel.

It was a place of dreams for me. It is the place in your mind that the child of your soul goes to when you are old and afraid. There were so many things at the lake house that were different from the city life of a child that I knew growing up: fishing, snakes, critters, turtles, country living, country people, things were just completely different. It was our happiness refuge. Everyone should have a place like this.

So smelling the burning smell when I sleep at night is not a bad experience for me. It tends to make me have good dreams. One night, the video store burned down about three hundred feet from my room from an electrical fire, which is common in Iraq. I had thought there was a strong smell but didn't investigate it until the next morning. Oh well, no one was hurt. The time was coming where I would soon be at home on leave with my family. My thoughts drifted to them. Soon I would be heading to central Baghdad to catch a flight to Kuwait and to return to the United States! §

19

There and Back Again

"Alice: Would you tell me, please, which way I ought to go from here?
The Cat: That depends a good deal on where you want to get to
Alice: I don't much care where.
The Cat: Then it doesn't much matter which way you go.
Alice: so long as I get somewhere.
The Cat: Oh, you're sure to do that, if only you walk long enough."
—Lewis Carroll, *Alice in Wonderland*

MONTH NINE

As I walked through the airport in Atlanta everyone clapped. It was a United Services Organization (USO) orchestrated event, but it was nice and everyone seemed to be really into it. For the Vietnam war veterans, this would have been an altogether different experience, with Americans spitting and throwing trash and calling service members baby killers. When you are a soldier you don't usually sit around thinking about how the public is going to welcome you in an airport. Although the gesture is nice and by far it is appropriate to honor those who serve, it is also an extremely draining experience.

It took two separate helicopter flights and three plane rides over the course of four days to travel home on my rest and recuperation leave (R and R). This time did not include waiting in terminals or in various makeshift military transient camps across the Middle East. My state of mind was awash with questions about how I should act and what I should say when I saw my family. I had talked to my wife on almost a daily basis and communicated by e-mail throughout my tour, but it just wasn't the same. We were both different, and we both knew this. With my military schools and this deployment, I had already been living away from my home for well over fifteen months, with several months left to go.

I couldn't go anywhere in the airports and terminals as I traveled without someone stopping me. Mostly they were middle-aged people, obviously emotional, and they would stop and say, "Thank you for your service." It was an incredibly nice gesture, but with my heightened state of emotion I just wanted to be left alone. Wearing my army combat uniform, I was a target for well-wishers. I was stressed out and needed to decompress badly.

There were many other soldiers in the airports traveling to various destinations across the United States. Finally, I had arrived at my last connecting flight that would take me to my hometown, where my wife would pick me up at the airport. A woman a few years older than me sat down and made small talk and then she thanked me also. Her approach was much different from those who had approached me up until now. I could barely control my emotions as we talked, and any mention of my family almost brought me to tears. She obviously understood this, because she had been a military brat whose father had served in Vietnam.

After I greeted my family, I was tagging along with my wife and walking around her work place and being greeted by more people wanting to say thanks. My wife's boss was a mutual friend and a retired colonel who had served in Vietnam. He felt vindicated by the fact that my experience was the exact opposite of his own. I did not want to be on the receiving end of any of this, but I respectfully abdicated and listened to him. Then it hit me.

This was why these people had to do this. Saying thank you to some random stranger wearing a uniform in an airport somehow atones for the actions of some ignorant people thirty-five years ago. It seems strange to me, but it seems perfectly normal to all the civilians friends I spoke to about it.

My wife cried deeply as I spoke to her before I prepared to return to Iraq following my two weeks of R and R leave. I told her that the man she had known was dead; he had died many, many months ago. Although I wanted so badly to connect with her, my kids, my life, it was not mine anymore. It was a gift and a privilege I no longer could count as my own. To even attempt to hold on to these things stirred emotions that I could not have. It is these thoughts and emotions that take you away from the place where you must be—here. "Here" is the endless combat missions, patrols, taskings, training, and other tasks associated with a tour in Iraq. Things were not in my hands anymore—not that they ever were. It is the act of holding on to this life, this existence, the pure act of possession that is the problem. None of these things are yours. It is the grand illusion that you somehow are, or ever were in charge of your life.

I had to do something to keep myself from being consumed with panic and fear about being placed in such a crazy situation with so many unknowns. What I viewed as my life, my existence, my place, was gone. So I chose to die inside. In a way, I chose a life without Hope. I could not leave my family, my home again, and even begin to develop a sense that things would ever be ok. I wondered if I would ever be this person again. I questioned whether the person I thought I was had really died, or perhaps was it that the person that I really am had just begun to live?

I had met people that thought this way, and I observed it at the time to be defeatist. Soldiers returned from months of combat, death, destruction, and burden. Am I different? What is it that separates me from them? Is it experience, training, or just the conscience decision to be more than what my environment decides that I should be? These tired people carry it in the eyes. You know it when you see their eyes. After all, as the saying goes, they are the windows to a man's soul.

Some people do take it too far and are more heavily afflicted than others. Combining this fatalism with ignorance is a recipe for disaster and recklessness. They are still young.

I knew a man who had been in Vietnam who and had been affected by the chemical Agent Orange. He was quiet, a chain smoker, and he had a weird look in his eyes. When I was a civilian and had no understanding of or association with the military I did not know what that look meant. I thought he looked like an afflicted, crazy person. Now I knew: Vietnam was his war. This was mine.

This is not the first time that military advisors and transition teams have been used. They were used in Vietnam by both the marines and the army. It is a task that is required after a large war or conflict, but it is one that is not always well thought through. The aftermath, what happens after the destruction—the fun stuff is over now. Now what?

My mid-tour leave was over now. I was rested, but not relaxed. My jaws were sore from the constant clenching of my teeth as I slept. The doctor explained to me that the extreme stress causes people to react in different ways. I came back with "post–R and R leave syndrome," an affliction that affects many of us. You are motivated and relaxed, having had a chance to de-stress and meet your family, your changed family—your friends, your changed friends. It is a little relaxing and very frustrating. My wife did an incredible job of making it a wonderful, although a little confusing, experience for me.

Morale on the team was low. Everyone was bickering, gossiping, and avoiding dealing with each other. They told me that it has always been this way. We had less than ninety days left at this point. Ninety days is nothing, I thought to myself. It was one of the final hurdles we were told about. That final hurdle is just getting through the last ninety days. One of the teams that we had observed when we came in did everything they could to avoid having to go on the roads and on combat missions for those last months. I don't blame them.

All had been quiet lately. It was easier to catch terrorists because they hate the cold. We did "snatch and grabs" in the early morning hours and would get them in their house while they were all cuddled up, nice and toasty, next to a kerosene heater. They weren't moving around to safe houses like they used to. Iraqis trusted the security forces more and more every day. The perception that everyone had was that the "surge" was working.

Our NP unit was better than when we started with them. Since I came back from leave we were working with a different American unit. I was only gone for a few weeks and so many things changed that I couldn't even count them all. Three new transition teams had moved in with us. Civilians had taken over many jobs around the base. There were rumors and stories of civilian contractors prostituting themselves who were kicked off the base while I was gone.

It was a very quiet time: no attacks, no EFPs, no IEDs. I should say few rockets, because one of the chow halls was hit with six rockets in the last couple of weeks. I try not to scare people too much when I relate my experiences to them. It just freaks them out. I hope that somehow by telling them a little about where we were hit or attacked, it might help them be more prepared for what could come, but they don't listen. They are, just as everyone who sees the news, subscribing to the idea that we are making progress. The veteran NCOs tell us that the Iraqis hate the cold, so the attacks go down in the winter.

One day it snowed! Only for a few minutes, but it was cold, and it was snowing! The Iraqis and the other foreign workers on the base were amazed by it. It was on the news, and they reported that it was the first time it had snowed in Baghdad since 1946!

It is a little like being Alice in Wonderland sometimes. Lots of strange things and people are around, trapped in a chain of events, with no idea which way to go, but still you are curious. Which way should we go from here? Somewhere. §

20

Fireball

"War is a curtain of dense black fabric across all the hopes and kindliness of mankind. Yet always it has let through some gleams of light, and not—I am not dreaming—it grows threadbare, and here and there and at a thousand points the light is breaking through."—H. G. Wells, *Mr. Britling Sees It Through*

MONTH ELEVEN—I AM ALONE ON THE SUPPLY BASE COORDINATING SUPPORT FOR THE TEAM. ALL HELL IS BREAKING LOOSE!

I walked out of the chow hall on a dark and smoky Iraqi night. I was on a supply mission away from the team again. The base I was on had been under attack on an almost daily basis for the last three days, so I was nervous. My team members were starting to joke that I was seeing more action than they were in combat because I was stuck in so many of these attacks on the supply base.

Whenever I left my living area on the supply base, I walked in such a manner that I was always close to something big, like a cement bunker, a vehicle, or a metal container, something I could duck under in case of an attack. This technique works, and I have had to use it so many times that I can't even remember, probably hundreds. Usually you get stuck in a cement bunker for about an hour or so while you wait to hear the all-clear signal. On this particular night the all-clear did not come for another twelve hours!

I walked and did my normal zigzag while looking for places to duck into when I saw the biggest fireball explosion that I have ever seen. I blinked from the blast and then watched as a chunk of metal a little larger than a golf ball moved past my face at eye level about two inches away. It was the same response you have when a fly or a bug comes at your face and you sense it. If my eyes had not been pointed in that direction anyway I would have walked into the chunk, and it would have caught me in the face.

I dropped to the ground and crawled on my belly past several twenty-foot shipping containers to a Bradley tank that was parked nearby. Clink! Clink-clink! Clunk! Clink-clink! That was the sound of the small and large pieces of metal as they struck the shipping container a foot over my head to my right. I jumped in the back of the tank along with several other soldiers, and we closed it up tight.

The clinking sounds were a little quieter from inside the tank, but we could still hear them hitting the tank's armor. We heard reports coming in over the radio about what was happening, mostly medical-related reports. One of the soldiers in the tank was a medic, and we thought we could see someone outside the tank that had been injured and was lying in the road. The medic jumped out and checked, but it was not a person, just pieces of something that had blown up. He came back, and then someone on the radio explained what was happening.

The large fireball explosion was from a five thousand gallon tanker of fuel that was hit with a rocket or a grenade. It was surrounded with cement barricades, but it still destroyed almost everything around it and caught another tanker on fire. The thick metal from the tanker blew into a million pieces, and one of them had flown right past my face!

This reminded me of a time during the first gulf war when I was a young soldier, and I was reading several books about the Vietnam war. We had no Internet or phones back then on a deployment so we read books. One of the books talked about walking in tank tracks or walking through areas where vehicles had driven or where people had already walked. My buddies in my unit made fun of me for practicing this. One day we had moved our camp to another site in southern Iraq and ended up in a minefield that we had to backtrack out of. The procedure required everyone to retrace their steps and reverse our vehicles back through the same tracks to get out of the minefield. My buddies never made fun of me again after that.

It was that experience that made me listen to the young sergeant who told me about walking closely to large barriers and vehicles early on in my tour in Iraq. He was right, and it surely had saved my life this day.

Half an hour later, several of us made our way back to the large building where the majority of the living quarters were arranged. It was getting late, and the enemy was getting started early tonight. We needed to hunker down in a well-protected building to ride out the evening and any attacks that would surely follow this one, which they did—with more rockets. *Lots* of rockets! I stacked up several metal wall lockers and some three-quarters-inch plywood at the head of my bunk and shut my eyes for a little while. Not more than twenty minutes later—BOOM!—a direct hit on the building. I opened my eyes but did not move. I could tell it was a direct hit because the cracks in the mortar in the ceiling let loose with some dirt and dust that slowly sifted down on me. I calmly rolled onto the floor and crawled low on my belly into the heavily protected inner hallway. It was only 9:00 or 10:00 pm at the time. All the residents of the building were huddled together in sleeping attire, talking and waiting to hear the next explosion.

Boom! Boom! Boom! Boom! Boom! Boom! That was six rockets. I got in the habit of counting the explosions, listening for direction, and type of explosion. Although I used to get excited by the explosions, I didn't anymore. It was useless to get worked up because you lose focus. The random explosions continued on for about another several hours. I got a message to the team at the outpost that I was okay and found out that they were also under attack. Things were going haywire all throughout our area. Iraqi police and army units were being dispatched all over the sector to stop the attacks.

A few miles away, a dump truck packed full of explosives pulled up to one of our Iraqi unit checkpoints. The Iraqi police were able to stop the truck and get the driver out. A senior Iraqi commander came to the scene and brought personnel that he claimed were trained in disarming explosives. In what had to have been a grisly scene, seven of the personnel climbed on the truck while others waited in close proximity. The truck blew up in a humongous explosion, killing fifteen Iraqi Policemen. Similar attacks on checkpoints continued throughout the night, along with the rocket attacks on us. It seemed like the enemy was just driving around in cars filled with portable rocket launchers.

It was just another day on the job working the supply issues. If you had asked me on this particular day if I thought my efforts in Iraq were worth the costs involved, you would have gotten a definitive "no." The attacks were all over the news. By the time I was able to contact my family back home everyone had heard about what had happened. I talked to my wife and told her I was alive and safe and out of harms way.

For now. §

21

Back to the Front

"A warrior considers himself already dead, so there is nothing to lose. The worst has already happened to him, therefore he's clear and calm; judging him by his acts or by his words, one would never suspect that he has witnessed everything."—Carlos Castaneda

As I was sitting in the hallway waiting on the rockets all night, I was sharing war stories with some friends and other soldiers I knew from other teams and other units. This is the custom in the army to try and outdo your buddies' stories with your own. Our stories really took on a new aspect because they were pretty dang serious and could be verified by the other people sitting around in the hallway. Sometimes you would hear a story second hand but hardly ever would you get first-hand accounts.

I was now getting so many first-hand accounts that I had decided to write them down in my journal. In retrospect, my duty as writer is to tell the story as best as possible and capture why it was important to be told. These stories are important because they are about real people. They are more than the fears and the dreams and the nightmares that we kept in our minds. These things could have easily happened to us on any day, but they happened to people we know. Here are six personal stories.

The Three Soldiers

Four soldiers were riding in an armored Humvee on a patrol with several other vehicles. They left in the morning as they had on many other quiet mornings, and had checked, double-checked, and triple-checked all equipment to travel outside the wire on a mission. This particular mission involved meeting some Iraqi counterparts at a predetermined meeting place. You had to be careful about what you told the Iraqis sometimes. You didn't want to give out too much information about what route you were going to take or where you were going to be. Suffice it to say that insurgents have numerous means of engaging us with nasty explosives, and today they engaged the lead vehicle.

Two of the soldiers in the first vehicle had their legs cut off and were killed as the vehicle was blown in half from an explosive. The fourth soldier was decapitated. No enemy was found. The team that this happened to was decimated and was unable to perform effectively after that incident. I had tried to contact and reach them for various reasons but they either didn't answer or were so focused on what had happened they could not assist me with routine business. You are never the same after something like that happens to you.

The Commo Guy

Earlier in the book I mentioned a communications sergeant with five kids who was killed and had been memorialized at Fort Riley. I spoke to members of his team who had been involved in the incident where he was killed. He and two others were killed in the attack, all burned to death inside of the Humvee when its doors would not open. The senior man and the gunner in the vehicle were struck but lived and were evacuated back to the United States to be treated. The other members in the convoy from the other vehicles were never the same after this incident.

Thanksgiving

We were at our combat outpost, it was close to thanksgiving. We were walking to the mobile kitchen trailer when we were stopped in our tracks by a large explosion outside of the post. It was pretty far away, but it was large enough for us to hear it. A lieutenant colonel had been traveling in a convoy up to our outpost when his vehicle was struck by an explosion. He survived, but his driver was decapitated and his gunner was killed.

A day or two later he was in our kitchen trailer, serving us thanksgiving dinner, as is the custom of army officers and senior noncommissioned officers during the holidays. A soldier confirmed this story, but I had seen the colonel myself. I knew what had happened to him but I could not make the words come out of my mouth. "I'm sorry," I thought when I looked at him. He had lost many soldiers, but this was different. He was in the same vehicle this time.

It was written all over his face. I looked at him only for a brief second as he served me some turkey. He was bravely conducting his duties, but death was all around him like a cloud hanging over a lake on a cold, foggy morning: sadness, anger, frustration, despair.

The Tower

Outposts normally have high walls with some type of observation tower on them, manned by security forces. You have to be extremely careful when you are on the towers because shooters will take potshots at you. I recalled an infantry soldier instructing us in our training when we were working in a building and searching it. He told us such precautions as to stay away from the windows, to go under them, to not smoke cigarettes, and so on. A cigarette can be seen for miles at night time on a clear night.

A soldier who was on duty on a tower in Iraq in our area one night was smoking near a window in the guard tower and was shot. He had made two mistakes: First, he silhouetted himself against the window. A dark shadow in a window is a pretty easy target. You keep your weapon trained on the window until the next time you see the shadow and then you shoot it. The second mistake he made was smoking the cigarette, which alerted the shooter in the darkness to his exact and fixed location.

The Bridge

Many months after my return from Iraq, I still would get very nervous near bridges. Bridges give the enemy the opportunity to shoot down into a vehicle or drop grenades or other explosives. One of the teams in our area lost a soldier to a rocket fired from the far side of a bridge as they passed underneath it. Driving under a bridge is a very predictable event. You are going under one side and are probably going to come out about the same spot on the other side. A technique we learned in training is to act crazy when you drive under the bridge and don't look so predictable. It is the lion and lamb concept: If you look like a lion and act a little crazy, an attacker will probably move on to someone who looks and acts more like a lamb. I always drove crazy under bridges to avoid this type of attack.

The Trail Vehicle

On our main supply base in the motor pool was a vehicle that was blown up and almost completely destroyed. It had crazy, large holes in it, and I remember passing by it on a few occasions and wondering what had happened to the people inside. I didn't realize until we were sitting in the hallway swapping stories that this was the same vehicle from our outgoing sister advisory team in another battalion. They were only a few weeks out from redeploying when the trail vehicle in their convoy was hit in the rear with a large explosive. All occupants survived, but several soldiers were injured and hospitalized.

In this war, the frontlines are everywhere. Many of the specific details of the incidents can not be shared, but as many as can be told are described here. It is the truth of the experience of Iraq during this time. These stories represent the experience of day-to-day transition team life in Iraq and what has come to define a tour in Iraq—it is what it is. §

22

The Interpreter

"Nothing in Iraq is what it seems … in Iraq this is the way of things"—Comment from an old Iraqi man on the street

END OF MONTH TEN—THIS IS THE END OF THE COLD MONTHS

"Frank was shot three times!" The interpreters stopped me in the hallway, visibly upset and speaking very loudly in their fragmented English, and told me that Frank had been shot. I asked them to slow down and explain what was going on. "Damn," I said. We had all hoped that Frank was going to be the one interpreter that we would get all the way through the system and get him his U.S. citizenship (a process that can take more than a year).

Frank, one of our interpreters (terps), was on leave and had gone home to give his pay to his family, as was the custom. There are no bank machines or online Internet banking here. Frank had been warning people that someone was watching and following him. All the Iraqis seemed to believe that people were watching them and following them all the time, so we really didn't pay much attention to it.

Frank is not his real name; none of the terps used their real names for security reasons. The terps are actually a bigger target than Americans because they are specifically targeted for helping the Americans. Since our tour had begun, we had seen several disturbing incidents involving the terps who worked with us, including some terps whose brothers had been killed or arrested and some who showed up for only a short time and then never returned.

The terps normally would go to great lengths to hide their identity, including wearing full-face masks and dressing in uniforms like soldiers.

Frank was now at an Iraqi hospital somewhere near where he lived in Baghdad. It sounds like a James Bond film to hear how the terps would switch cars, switch taxis, backtrack on themselves, and so on to try to avoid being tracked back to their homes. We did not know it at the time, but Frank was actually at a hospital run by the Jeesh al-Mahdi (JAM).

He had been at the hospital for about an hour, bleeding to death. He had a collapsed lung, and had been shot in the chest, hand, and in the leg. Iraqi hospitals can do very little to treat someone in this condition.

Our operations officer, Captain Doug Zabalinski (Z), our team medic Staff Sergeant Lott (Doc), and our team chief began making phone calls. The bottom line was that Frank had to get to a coalition forces hospital in the next hour or he was going to die.

At the time, no one knew the policy for treating terps in U.S. facilities. This is when Doc jumped in. "I think I can get Frank into a hospital in the International Zone if we can just get him there somehow." Driving was out of the question. Our brigade team was very close to where Frank was currently located, and he could have been brought there and stabilized at the aid station. They didn't want to help us at all. As a matter of fact, all they had to do was meet Frank at the gate and get him in to the aid station, but they wouldn't do it. We moved on to other options.

The phone calls continued as we waited nervously for updates on the situation. At this point, the team chief and Z called our NP battalion commander and asked for his assistance. They had complete freedom of movement around Baghdad and Sadr City since they were from Iraq and they live here, whereas we aren't, and we don't.

Our NP commander was extremely helpful and coordinated for the brigade ambulance to be escorted by several of the NPs. We later learned that when the Iraqi platoon leader went in to get Frank from the Iraqi hospital, they were about to operate on him. It was a JAM hospital and a JAM doctor, and if they had known that Frank was a terp, they would have killed him. He probably would have died from their surgery anyway, even if they were trying to save him.

Usually the fight was with bullets, but this time the fight was with the bureaucracy. Doc mentioned that usually his hands were bloody from assisting directly in helping to save someone's life. Now he was making phone calls and coordinating to save Frank. The case was complicated, but in the end the people at the hospital will err on the side of keeping the person alive. Doc got the approval to get Frank into the hospital in the international zone. Now we had to get him there. At this point, Z got on the phone with the gate guards and explained the situation to them. The NP convoy and the ambulance proceeded to the hospital in the IZ. The staff there was waiting and immediately grabbed Frank like any hospital emergency room in the United States would have done for a gunshot wound patient that had come in to the emergency room. Stabilize the patient; then ask the questions.

This is the way it is in Iraq. The American systems work, but Iraqi systems are hit or miss. You are on the ground with an Iraqi unit in a transition team. You are supposed to help get their systems working, but the people telling you to do this sit in big, secure offices with e-mail, phones, and a soda machine. They eat in big, nice chow halls and live in their own trailer. They want you to somehow miraculously start making things work from the bottom up. In other words, they don't have a clue what is really going on, nor do they want to know. Meanwhile, you have all sorts of bureaucracy on both the U.S. side and the Iraqi side to fight through. It is a wonder anything over here gets accomplished. I dealt with this daily in my logistics duties.

Iraqis cannot automatically be treated in a U.S. facility. The terps work for Titan International and do not have any form of health insurance. Iraqi hospitals are not able to take care of basic problems of health treatment so they definitely can't treat gunshot wounds.

Frank lived. We got a couple of updates: He started out in critical condition and eventually improved to the point that he was moved to a ward and eventually released.

Our interpreters were upset throughout the whole drama. In the end, they were relieved a little bit when they saw the great lengths that we went to for Frank. We treated him as a member of the team. The NP worked with us as a member of their team. We had never had to rely on them so much as we did on that day.

That is the irony. We are helping them all the time to improve, but they are helping us too. Sometimes the greatest help to ever give to someone is to help them discover who they really are. We buy them supplies; we coordinate for equipment for operations. Every day they get a little better. Many times, police had been shot and treated at U.S. facilities or evacuated by U.S. forces. What would you do? How would you act? Knowing that you faced impossible obstacles to save someone's life that you didn't have to save, would you save them? Our NPs did this for us, for Frank, when our own brigade unit would not even walk to the gate to meet the ambulance and bring it in.

There is a common bond between all of us. We all have different roles and jobs but the bond is the same. Terps, Iraqi NP, infantry security guys, transition team members—war creates the strangest of friends. There is a question we all have. It is a little thing that no one can talk about but we all secretly carry it in our soul. People who possess strength of character no matter what role they have will get it right. The question is about loyalty? Not to God, not to country, not to JAM, not to the police, or the army, but to one another.

When we are bleeding, with three bullets in our body, we all want the same thing—to be taken care of by those with whom we have lived, and worked, and trained, and fought. You want the loyalty that you have given to be returned to you in the moment that you need it most. §

23

The Counterpart

> "All men dream, but not equally. Those who dream by night in the dusty recesses of their minds wake in the day to find that it was vanity: but the dreamers of the day are dangerous men, for they may act their dream with open eyes, to make it possible."—T. E. Lawrence

"Maj Zuhair, come here!" Sadie (a respectful way of saying sir to a senior-ranking Iraqi) rang the little doorbell on his desk, and one of the many assistants he had went to summon Major Zuhair from his office/personal room. "Sadie, did you say Major Zuhair? I thought he was out of the NPs."

Two weeks before, they were talking about "disappearing" Major Zuhair. I had to stop and ask him what they meant by that (I was thinking of a one-way trip in the trunk of a black Mercedes). "No, no … he is being 'disappeared' off of the roles of the National Police. We had a translation miscommunication." "Okay," I said.

Sadie went on to explain to me how he had a meeting with Major Zuhair and had shown him the error of his ways. He had explained to Major Zuhair that he would always be on the run, trying to avoid being put in jail and would have no way to take care of his family. Major Zuhair had a family member that was sick and he needed the money. Major Zuhair was one of the few holdovers from the previous regime of the previous commanding officers. He wasn't real proactive but he was careful; he had been around for a while as a supply officer, which is not an easy task in Iraq. Supply officers often take the brunt of their commander's anger about an inefficient and inadequate system of supplies and equipment.

The team chief was on leave and I was sitting in Sadie's office late in the evening having chai (bitter, hot, orange-flavored tea with about two pounds of sugar in a two ounce glass). This was often the case with Sadie. We would discuss all sorts of things about operations, intelligence, supplies, money, and so forth. He would ring the little doorbell on his desk whenever he thought he needed to talk to a particular person. He was a good battalion commander, but he did almost everything himself while his executive officer (XO) sat over in the office across the hall smoking the hookah (a water pipe). Such is the way in Iraq.

There were at least four counterparts that I had to interact with besides Sadie in the battalion to advise and assist our battalion. One officer was in charge of the trucks. Another was in charge of the supplies, ammunition, and weapons. A third was in charge of submitting the administrative requests from the battalion (all of them). And the executive officer (XO) was supposed to oversee this stuff. I was also the XO of the team, so I was supposed to advise him, too. Many of the policemen could not read or write much less use a computer. When we started, they had three computers, none of which worked. We'd come a long way since then in a short time.

Major Zuhair was the senior logistics guy. But he didn't want to touch anything or do anything without the commander's approval. (Later I figured out why.) Major Zuhair had been absent without leave (AWOL) so many times lately that I had stopped even asking about him. The majority of tasks I dealt with were controlled directly by the commander anyway, so I dealt with him most of the time. This was the "commander-centric" approach used by many Iraqi commanders, especially when it came to supplies.

My initial attempts to deal with Major Zuhair were textbook. They were exactly by the training I had received, but I started to notice that the NP were reluctant to give out any information about the battalion. We dug in later and found out why. Many weapons were missing and unaccounted for. Policemen would just quit and go home and take the weapons with them. The new battalion commander was as amazed as we were at the whole situation. I backed off and asked him about his family and things would go better with the conversation. Later on, we took a different approach and got a good status on all the weapons.

The first thing Sadie did was walk us around the entire battalion and point things out to us. We both had the same look in our eyes, disgust. The lack of discipline and inattention in this place was beyond words. It was dirty, it was smashed, it was thwarted;

it was bad. I wrote everything down with the team chief. Every defininciency that I noted Sadie had corrected within a week. He impressed me. I decided to help him out as much as I possibly could.

I spent the next several months helping to obtain funding and equipment to get them up to a basic standard of living and operations. This is not an easy task with the NP. Many people have written the NP off and only focus on helping the Iraqi Army. Instead of telling you the truth, they use a standard party line with you. I call them the HTA police. That is the acronym I came up with for staff and senior officers and NCOs who, instead of doing something to help the Iraqis, say, "You need to hold them accountable." I had so many people tell me this that I started using the HTA acronym. But it didn't stop me. It just made me mad.

Many transition teams stop right there. If they are told no, then they go back to the barracks and that is it. They ride the tour out with the same words echoing every time their unit needs something instead of helping them to get the stuff—HTA.

This was our unit—*our* unit. Maybe that was the American in me coming out, but I liked this unit and the commander, and I wanted to see them succeed. They pretty much needed everything. They were living a lot like we did in billeting with cheap beds and mattresses. By the time we were done, you could have taken an American Army unit in and had it operate and live in the place. The first thing we did was get the operations room up and running, and next we got accountability of the weapons and then the property.

Nothing is more frustrating than purchasing items for the Iraqis and then a month later nobody knows what happened to the stuff. I made a habit of taking lots of pictures and having them sign hand receipts for common supplies, showing them accountability. Sadie helped with this, and I was confident that they were properly accounting for supplies after reviewing the newly established property book.

It is an old leadership lesson. that the most powerful teacher you have is your example. We learned this lesson through the NCOs on our team. We ran a little month-long training course for the quick reaction platoon. It was very frustrating by American standards. Police would show up late or not show up; NCOs did not enforce standards. Officers did nothing to support the training.

Our NCOs conducted the majority of the training, and by the end of the it the NCOs they were working with were actually acting like NCOs, whereas before they didn't even wear their rank and we could hardly ever even get guys to show up in uniform. The example that our NCOs set was seen and experienced by the policemen and the NCOs on a daily basis, and it began to be emulated.

The weapons accountability thing blew up when the brigade commander came down and did an inspection. He really just came down to chew Major Zuhair's butt a little bit and make an example of him. He went overboard with it and ended up telling Major Zuhair that he was going to put him in jail. I tried to hide it, but I realized I was rolling my eyes when the man was talking. This guy was blaming everything that was wrong with this unit on one guy, the scapegoat. I figured out what was going on, and later the battalion commander told me that he had done this on purpose to get the guy's attention.

So guess what happened? He went AWOL. Imagine that. I had asked Sadie not to fire him because Sadie had been firing about an officer a day in trying to clean house—a good thing, we later realized. Most of the officers were kind of like country bumpkins with no real managerial or leadership skills and were just wasting space.

One day we had had several distinguished visitors to the battalion, what is commonly referred to as "the model' or standard for the division and the brigade. Sadie brought in Iraqi generals from both the NP and the Iraq Army on a regular basis to talk shop. He was proud of the conditions around the battalion and so were we. Many systemic issues still existed but they were endemic to the problems with the Ministry of the Interior and the level of corruption that exists.

The battalion, our battalion, was one to be proud of. The morale of the unit had improved and the corrupt members were at least lying low. All the property in the battalion was accounted for and several systems were in place.

In many units in our army staff officers carried around a little memory stick on a lanyard around their neck to pass along big files, briefings, and so on. I was watching the interaction between some of the staff and the admin guys one day. They were walking around with memory sticks, comparing notes, and preparing briefings. I smiled. It reminded me of being in an American unit again. That was a good thing. §

24

VALOR

"For exceptionally meritorious achievement by going above and beyond the call of duty under hostile fire ... SSG Lott led a team of six personnel during the JAM offensive ..."—Doc's award citation. It is preceded by the word VALOR in all caps. Doc saved several people.

MONTH TWELVE

Doc was very busy as we prepared to leave Iraq in the last month of our tour. We always joked with him about this issue because he was usually not the busiest person on the team. He would reply with something like, "I can assure you that the medic not being busy is a good thing." Doc was right. I had been flying around Iraq and coordinating accounts and support for the incoming new team. I had been at the supply base when the increased attacks by the Jeesh al-Mahdi began. Our outpost was the closest installation in the area for many U.S. soldiers and the Iraqi military. Therefore, our helipad and medical station were a conduit to life-saving medical support on larger posts with big hospitals.

The first ten to fifteen minutes after a major injury is critical to saving a person's life, and Doc knew this. Roughly one-third of deaths occur in the first minutes of a major injury, and the majority of patients who can actually make it to the big hospital alive will survive. It is the making it to the hospital part that is hard in combat. You are so far away from specialized medical care that it can take a half an hour to get you there.

Doc was instrumental in saving eight lives with pretty serious injuries during this time. Doc is a staff sergeant. and he was the senior medic on our installation. He took charge of the medics during the increase in attacks and coordinated the ground medical support, prioritized patients with various types of injuries, and supervised the evacuation by helicopter of numerous patients with serious combat wounds.

Doc didn't talk about it too much after we got back, and things really got crazy in those last days before we left, so I missed out on a great deal of the details. It was many months later that I heard about an award for Doc that had been upgraded to an Army Commendation medal with "Valor" that I realized how much he had done at the time. An award with Valor is rare. The brigade commander of the U.S. forces in the area appropriately recognized what were obvious acts of valor on Doc's part and forwarded the award to Master Sergeant Calderon a few months later.

The outpost was under attack about every other day by small arms fire, mortars, and rockets. Doc was splitting his time between working on our team and coordinating the medical operations at our little medical station on the outpost that we shared with other units. The attacks got worse in our final days in Iraq—much worse.

In one incident, an Iraqi officer was shot several times in the abdomen during a nasty firefight, and doc treated him, stabilized him, and evacuated him for further treatment. I don't remember which patient it was, but I do remember witnessing one medical evacuation with Doc.

I was working on getting the Iraqis some additional food and water because the sustained combat had them running low on critical supplies. I was working with a young soldier loading some supplies. We started to take small arms fire, and a few mortar rounds exploded very close to us. We immediately dropped to the ground and squeezed up under a nearby twenty-foot shipping container that was sitting on some large bricks. The rounds were so close the pieces of shrapnel were spraying across the container extremely loud. After the attack I walked by the main gate that led out to the helipad and witnessed Doc riding on the hood of a Humvee holding an I.V. bag high in the air in one hand and covering a patient on a stretcher with the rest of his body so that the sand from the choppers wouldn't get in the wounds of the patient as he was loaded onto the evacuation helicopter.

I was proud of Doc and was extremely happy that he was a highly competent medic. A soldier will go the extra mile and do some heroic things they wouldn't normally do when they know that they will be taken care of by a good medic if they are injured. In another incident, several U.S. soldiers were hit with shrapnel from a large explosion and had wounds all over the arms, legs, and chest areas. Doc stabilized them and evacuated them quickly. Another patient came in during one of the attacks with his skull split open from a gunshot wound. The patient was Iraqi, and Doc got an interpreter and then spoke to the patient to calm him down. Doc then treated him, stabilized him, and had him evacuated to the hospital.

In all these scenarios, Doc was running around making these things happen while incoming rounds and small arms fire were going off all around him. Death and destruction surround the team all the time during this period. Blown-up vehicles were parked everywhere on the outpost, waiting to be sent back to the rear for repair. They had rocket holes, flat tires, and bullet holes. Buildings had impact points and cracks in them from bullets and explosions. The satellite dish receiver looked like a piece of Swiss cheese.

It seemed as though we had not been cut any breaks on this tour to Iraq. Why should we expect any now? As you get closer to returning home, you begin to feel you will awake from the bad dream. Time slows down. Each day begins to seem like a week, and each week seems more like a month. You start to think about the things that gave you hope when you started the tour, like your life after Iraq, your family, imagining what things would be like. This may sound perfectly normal, and it is. These are dangerous thoughts in a situation like the one we were in because they cause you to lose focus. When you lose focus, you make mistakes. When you make mistakes in combat, people die. §

25

The Offensive

MONTH TWELVE—FOURTEEN DAYS TO GO!

It is the second day since the Jeesh al-Mahdi attacked Sadr City in one of the biggest offensives in years. The Iraqi battalion executive officer (my current Iraqi counterpart) is dead, shot in the back of the head at one of the checkpoints in Sadr City. My anxiety level is as high as I can ever remember. My thoughts are clouded with the strange dreams (more like nightmares) and the restless sleep from multiple nights of listening to barrages of incoming and outgoing mortars, artillery, and rockets firing. The battalion security officer from the Iraqi battalion stops at our building at 3:00 am to inform us that Jeesh al-Mahdi elements are attacking the perimeter. The buzz of multiple large-caliber automatic weapons in the distance confirms his report. Exactly two weeks are left until we redeploy. Our replacements are on the ground in Iraq but they cannot get to us because all the helicopters are being diverted in direct support of combat operations. I wonder aloud to myself, is this all just a really long, bad dream? If so, how do I wake myself up? Pinching doesn't work. This must be real.

Our preparations for redeployment are halted amidst the chaos. Our replacements are due in any time now. Questions are arising about whether they will be able to make it in by helicopter to our outpost because of the chaos and the attacks. We are as far out on the frontier as any Americans in the country are stationed, with the exception of the transition teams that sit out on the Syrian and Iranian borders.

In the last month and a half of our tour in Iraq, we were transferred from advising our NP unit to advising a newly formed battalion of the Iraq Army. We had observed them as they arrived in Hope with all of their new equipment and wondered about the new situation of having them around the outpost. Their advisor team was internally formed, meaning their equipment and personnel were taken from within an existing army unit in Iraq, unlike our team, which was specifically formed and trained in the United States as a transition team.

The newly formed internal team was hardly able to get their stuff together and sustain themselves. They were so busy with their own issues that they had barely interacted with the unit. We were viewed as being more seasoned and properly equipped to handle our advising duties, so a request was sent—allegedly, all the way up to General Petraeus—to have us switched over. We had developed our NP unit about as far as they were going to go without any further equipment and supply assistance. They had formed into a pretty decent unit in the months that we spent with them. The Iraqi Army Battalion was a whole different story.

News reports the previous day stated that civilians were observing elements of the Jeesh al-Mahdi pre-positioning weapons, ammunition, and rockets, inside mosques throughout the area. They use ambulances to subversively transport these contraband items to various caches for future use. Jeesh al-Mahdi techniques were to fight in an area for a short period, then move to another area where they had stored weapons and ammo, and then blend into the populace so we couldn't find them. It was pretty effective. Hiding weapons in mosques, using ambulances to transport weapons, torturing and killing innocent civilians, fighting as an armed force without uniforms—these are all clear violations of the Geneva and Hague Conventions and the Law of War. Unfortunately, Jeesh al-Mahdi is not well versed in international law.

In our area, the attacks had begun on the western side two days ago and progressed throughout to our front doorstep on the eastern side. Jeesh al-Mahdi elements were attacking and taking over checkpoints in force with more firepower than the guards and elements manning the checkpoints. Some reports said they had kidnapped Iraqi Army soldiers and were using stolen uniforms, equipment, and vehicles to attack. Other reports said that IPs (Iraqi Police) were involved. One report said that Jeesh al-Mahdi members were telling the Iraqi soldiers to abandon the checkpoints immediately or they would be killed. Some of the Iraqi *jundi* (soldiers) said they observed Iraqi police in the mix assisting the JAM, and they had screamed at them, "Where are you going to go? What are you going to do? JAM is the police!"

As the Iraqi Army Battalion began to lose soldiers to the fighting, things really got out of control.

The fighting continued to progress to the point where all of the checkpoints were lost and subsequently abandoned, allowing Jeesh al-Mahdi freedom of movement throughout the area and into other areas of Iraq. We didn't know it at the time, but things were going crazy all over Iraq in what was apparently a preplanned, coordinated multipronged attack. The other main area of attack was in Basrah, where related elements of Jeesh al-Mahdi were taking over the city. Sketchy television reports stated that multiple air strikes against Basrah had been launched and a time limit of seventy-two hours was issued to have the city cleared or it would be assaulted in force. Later reports in the newspapers confirmed that the Iraqi Army in Basrah had similar circumstances, with more than thirteen hundred soldiers and policemen fired for deciding to sit out the battle.

We began tracking the battle of our unit in our operations center as the reports began to come in. By the time the battalion XO's body was brought back to base, several more Iraqi soldiers had been killed or injured. Up to half of our Iraqi battalion had fled, been captured, were killed, or could otherwise not be accounted for. Our Iraqi Army Battalion was almost out of ammunition and had run out of food. The personnel numbers were now down to under a 150 soldiers by the end of day two. Iraqi Army soldiers who were manning a checkpoint in the southern area of Sadr City were hiding out in a building with wounded *jundi* and no ammunition. They needed help. What a mess.

Coalition forces were busy with attacks all over Baghdad and were unable to lend much support to our battalion. The Jeesh al-Mahdi Special Groups was using similar tactics to those that had been used in 2004. They would fire and then immediately mix themselves in with civilian crowds. This rendered our forces unable to engage with Apache attack helicopters, armored vehicles, or smaller caliber weapons. Jeesh al-Mahdi used hospitals and mosques to hide large caches of weapons and ammunition and to house combatants. We had reports that the hospital closest to one of our checkpoints was being used as a base of operations for a JAM special groups company. Again, what a mess.

It seemed that every time the coalition forces attempted to maneuver around Sadr City the units would run into explosive devices. We unfortunately witnessed the aftermath of the helicopters as they came screaming in to our small combat outpost. Ours was the closest helipad in the area with medical support near to stabilize a patient, get them on a bird, and get them into surgery in central Baghdad as quickly as possible. Over the course of a couple of days, we witnessed numerous vehicles completely destroyed by rocket-propelled grenades, incoming mortar fire, and EFPs. Many of the soldiers made it through with injuries that they will eventually be able to overcome. Some were not so lucky. In one particularly gruesome scene, a convoy came in to get some soldiers being evacuated for medical support. The lead vehicle, a heavily armored route clearance vehicle, had taken a direct hit with a highly explosive device with a large explosive yield. One soldier's body parts were all over the vehicle, and it was the type of scene that haunts your dreams forever. There would be more scenes like this in days to come. Our replacements could not get in fast enough.

We integrated ourselves with the Iraqi battalion operations center with interpreters to get a picture of what was going on and to provide a liaison between the unit and the coalition forces. We didn't know it at the time, but coalition forces were so heavily engaged they could provide little assistance.

After several hours of broken reports from screaming Iraqi soldiers on the radio, the battle focused on two areas of fighting, primarily with interspersed engagements throughout the area, including our outpost. The first area was a square in the southwestern area (actually, it was a traffic circle) and an important checkpoint in the northern area. The square was adjacent to the Badr Corporation headquarters and was a popular area for Jeesh al-Mahdi attacks. Badr Corporation was a front organization for various JAM organizations (they control parts of the government, various corporations, and hospitals). The infighting within JAM had grown in the last couple of months with various portions disobeying orders from Sadr and launching their own initiatives after Sadr had ordered to continue the ceasefire.

About three months ago, this same area was the scene of an intense battle between Jeesh al-Mahdi elements and the Badr Corporation, with our NP unit providing assistance. Several NP units, Iraqi Army units, and coalition forces units engaged a significant JAM force at this location. Using Iraqi tanks, coalition forces air support, and ground security, the situation was controlled. Now it was out of control—with one of our Iraqi units pinned down, surrounded on all sides by JAM with no coalition forces to assist them.

We were sitting in the office of the Headquarters Company Commander, who was now the de facto battalion XO, when the news about the cease-fire came on the TV. Our battalion commander had proven to be extremely ineffective as a commander. He disobeyed any orders to engage his forces from his infantry battalion into further combat. This resulted in several fistfights that we witnessed between the brigade commander and the battalion commander. We were in the process of recommending up the American chain that he be relieved immediately. We actually recorded him on video stating that he would not send any of his soldiers into harm's way. Then he would turn around and ask for coalition forces support. We could not get rid of this guy fast enough.

Muqtada al-Sadr issued a statement on the news about the cease-fire, and the Iraqis around the battalion began to fire off celebratory gunfire. This is an extremely nerve-wracking event, for a U.S. soldier to witness fifty or more Iraqi soldiers firing their weapons in the air wildly. Our standards of discipline would have ensured that each one of those soldiers was punished, yet this was normal for them.

The offensive had left our Iraqi battalion at a third of its normal strength without a battalion commander or an XO. One of the company commanders was in jail for refusing to fight (and he was the best officer they had). Numerous weapons and vehicles were destroyed, captured, or missing, and much of it was now in use by Jeesh al-Mahdi Special Groups in Sadr City. Reports were now coming in that JAM were seen walking the streets in Sadr City with Iraqi Army M16s (ones that we had issued to them upon graduation from Iraqi basic training).

By the end of the sixth day, all of the checkpoints were retaken by the Iraqi Army after much prodding by coalition forces and higher-ups in the Iraqi chain of command. Dozens of coalition forces vehicles were out of commission. More than twenty coalition forces soldiers on our outpost were killed or wounded. We were wearing our body armor and gear all the time now. We later learned that Basrah had similar experiences with JAM attacking in the area and that the Iraqi Army and police had performed similarly.

We accompanied the Iraqi Army on one particular mission that none of us will ever forget. We had barely made it out of the gate when the Iraqis began to circle the wagons. In this maneuver, they were driving around the convoy in circles, shooting wildly in all directions. We had not been fired at by anyone or anything that our team could identify. The Iraqis were scared out of their minds. Later we were parked adjacent to an Iraqi Army checkpoint when several of the soldiers began shooting at something down the road. At first we could not make out what they were shooting at but then we could see children about two hundred meters down the road. Thank God the kids were fast runners. The checkpoint was opening up on anything that moved. The convoy continued on.

Fourteen days to go … §

Author note - The events in this chapter are now referred to as the "Battle of Sadr City" or "The JAM Offensive."

26

The Nightmare

"Hope is the dream of a waking man."—Aristotle

Four days to go. The climax of our yearlong story was not going to end peacefully—quite the opposite. It was going to be a sprint to the finish line for all of us. The prize of this race – was that you got to go home alive. The nightmare year of all of our lives was not going to end just yet.

The amount of people packed into the building was doubled when the new team arrived. We had the schedule arranged down to the minute, because we had to. There was no time to waste. There were so many things to do and not enough time to do them in. This is called a RIPTOA (Relief in Place or Transfer of Authority), where an outgoing unit trains and overlaps with a new incoming unit to replace them. The new team brought with them an infusion of new ideas … they were fresh. We were not.

We had just been through a weeklong JAM offensive that was arguably one of the most stressful times of the entire year, and people were sensitive about everything. In preparation for the next day, we were to get our mission brief the night before we were going on our "left seat ride." This is where we show them how to do it. Then on the next mission, they do the mission and we just kind of advise them (the "right seat ride").

Unfortunately, this area was hot (enemy active) and no transition teams had ever been to the checkpoint we were going to for the mission. The checkpoint was one that was overrun within hours of the JAM offensive. We were to convoy out with a platoon of American vehicles. A brand-new Iraqi battalion commander and two of their armored Humvees would accompany us.

Adding to the stress and intensity of the day, the mission changed three times from when it was briefed the night before until the next day when they left on the mission. We also knew that every convoy that had left the gate in the last ten days had been hit by an RPG, an IED. or EFP, or was engaged by mortars and small arms fire. We were sure to get hit.

Doing a mission like this in such a hot environment with new people is probably the most dangerous type of mission that you could do. As usual, the Iraqis were late to the mission, so we left for the mission at 1330. We drove through *mulhallas* just outside of our outpost, a little over halfway to the checkpoint. It was a typical scene in Sadr City—impoverished and desperate people everywhere lacking in the basic necessities. The streets were filled with barefoot, dirty kids, clapping and asking for water and food, but the kids were giving us the thumbs up. This was a good sign that the neighborhood was friendly toward us. If they were flipping us off or throwing rocks, you could expect an IED or EFP on the way back from the mission.

After a great deal of carefully traveling through various neighborhoods, we arrived at the checkpoint, and the situation on the ground was completely different from what we had thought. This caused us to adjust our plan and vehicle placement before we dismounted. We ended up staying for more than forty-five minutes, much longer than we had expected to. The army lieutenant colonel traveling with us seemed bent on exposing us to unnecessary risk at every possible juncture. Our team's perception of him was that he was looking for a fight.

The Iraqi soldiers at the checkpoints were in mix-matched uniforms. Their weapons were dirty. They hadn't had water in a couple of days and were drinking the water out of the drainage ditch nearby. The ditch was absorbing runoff from a pretty nasty garbage dump nearby, so of course they were sick with dysentery. I was particularly pissed off about this because we were providing purified water on a daily basis to the battalion in tanks, and we had even supplied bottled water to take to the checkpoints. All the Iraqis had to do was take the water out to the checkpoints, but they obviously had not.

There was no tactical consideration to the layout of the checkpoint. If JAM were to attack again, they would easily overrun the checkpoint. We took pictures and shook hands and spoke to the *jundi,* and the medics gave them medicine for the dysentery. We gave the checkpoint all the food and water we could, and there was a lot of talk among *jundi* that the unit didn't care about them. The new battalion commander delivered a good speech to them and made a lot of promises. The *jundi* seemed hopeful by the time that we left.

These checkpoints were the ones that our old NP battalion commander had laughed at when we told him that we were going to them. He had laughed and said, "This area is *very dangerous*. If you go in, do not take the same way back. They will place IEDs all along the road. This area is where a battalion of JAM lives and operates, and this is where they bring in all the EFPs from Iran." Great news. ...

We now had no choice on how to return, so we were forced to go back the way we came, but the kids were still out, so we had a good feeling. As we approached the main entrance to the gate of our outpost, the new Iraqi battalion commander wanted to continue on to two new checkpoints farther down the road. From three similar circumstances, in which we had been traveling with other elements who also had then decided to "push on" for whatever reason, our experience had taught us: all three times, they were hit with IEDs. The convoys are watched, and when they see you go out, they put IEDs on avenues and roads that you would then likely travel. We weren't going. Sure enough, a few minutes later we heard the unmistakably close sounds of the convoy being attacked by RPGs and small arms fire.

The next day was the right seat ride, when the new team would lead the mission. We were only going along to advise them on this one. It was clear from the intelligence reports that the convoy was definitely going to be hit that day. It was briefed that we had to go out to demonstrate to the Iraqis that we were willing to fight along side them. This time, there would be no platoon of U.S. support. What *great* news!

Not soon after leaving "the wire," we were engaged from the rear by an RPG from about four hundred meters. This missed the vehicles and exploded nearby, and we immediately began to receive small arms fire. A few minutes later, we felt the heavy, unmistakable thuds of enemy mortar rounds as they began to impact around the vehicles. The bad guys were definitely prepared for this.

The Iraqi Army soldiers and our soldiers all returned fire, and we positioned our vehicles in a defensive perimeter. The JAM guys were very good at firing and then blending into the area so you had to have positive identification before engaging anything with your weapon, which is not a very easy task to accomplish in practice.

Back at our outpost, the mortars section was preparing to drop some rounds on the enemy currently surrounding us. Within minutes of the beginning of the firefight, friendly mortar rounds began landing in the distance at likely enemy positions, which the Americans had preplanned (thank God). We continued to get sporadic small arms fire for the next several minutes when the Iraqi commander then announced that he was returning to outpost Hope with his *jundi*, However, the army lieutenant colonel who was with us had something else in mind.

The colonel said, "We have not identified any enemy or shot anyone yet; we are staying out here." Against the advice of every senior NCO on the ground and two field grade officers we were ordered to remain, we ended up staying for about ten more minutes. We took cover and attempted to positively identify any enemy while we could see and hear the small arms landing around us. Because of the layout of the buildings, we were unable to identify any enemy without hitting the civilians living in the buildings.

During this time, the colonel was standing out in the middle of the road. No kidding! He either thought he was invincible or he just had a death wish and wanted to get shot so he could get his Purple Heart. His NCOs (two master sergeants each with more than eighteen years of service) could be heard screaming profanities to get him down behind cover.

Finally, the colonel decided that it was time to go back. Everyone remounted and returned to the outpost without further incident. The mood in the vehicles was of disbelief. Our guys had never before felt happier that they were leaving. This reckless leadership was sure to continue on after we left. We felt a little guilty that we had to leave the new team in a situation like this.

We continued to advise and close out the RIPTOA. The new team was pretty happy in the end, and they thanked us for giving the best RIPTOA possible. During this time, our scheduled flights out of Hope were cancelled and then rescheduled three times, which contributed to continuing to beat down our morale and motivation. We were done with our mission, but we still couldn't get out of their and go home. Finally we made it out. Many of the team members said that as they flew away from Hope, it felt as if a heavy weight was lifted off. Others said it was like somebody getting out of prison … a really bad prison.

My feelings are that it was like a bad dream, the same way that you feel when the familiar lingering, dreaded feeling still carries over with you as you wake from a nightmare. The weight of being done with such a monumental and hellacious task was lifted but we still feel dirty somehow, as if affected by the things we were exposed to. How can you not feel that? You just can't shake it off.

We were waiting on our flight to take us away from Iraq (hopefully forever). Our souls were different now. Everyone was quiet. We did not yell and celebrate like the other soldiers waiting for flights. Our thoughts were mixed with worries about the past and the future. What would happen to the Iraqi battalion, the terps that were like our sons and brothers, and the new team that we left there? What about the families of all those fallen soldiers? What did our futures hold with the people we left behind for so long and we who we hadn't been able to think about? Some would say that from experiences like this you can take away good things and grow from them. We didn't say that at all. We didn't ask the questions that we used to ask, "Why are we doing this?" and "Why are these soldiers dying?" We were just glad to be leaving … alive.

This is the nightmare. Maybe nightmares are useful in a way. They powerfully remind you of something that was not meant to be forgotten. You want to forget it because you have to, to go on with your life—the life you have been away from for so long. No matter how terrible or awful it all seems, these things should not be forgotten. Iraq should never be forgotten.

Maybe at least for a few years, these things will not be remembered, and some day, some faraway day, we can take this book out and remember them … but not until the dreams of hope are gone forever. §

Epilogue

In a quiet moment of contemplation, I sat on the small chair on the front porch of my home and enjoyed the wistful smoke from my Montecristo cigar. I was watching the sprinkler in my front yard as it "tick, tick, ticked" across the fresh green grass. The family was out late, running some errands, on this particular dark and rainy fall Saturday evening. In the background, the familiar sounds of the trains passing by on the tracks a mile from my house reminded me of why it was good to be home. It was now six months after my return from Iraq. My mind drifted back to the quiet moments like this, when I would sit outside the building in Iraq in the late evening thinking about what I would write the next morning. Quiet moments like these are rare nowadays.

The family was all together again. As my daughter often mentions, "My family is all here." She is excited because I am home from Iraq after almost two years away from home. Also, my oldest son is now back from his job, working at a paper mill for several months while I was deployed. My time now is spent putting the finishing touches on this book and getting it ready to turn in.

Now and then, the team sends funny e-mails to each other, and I find myself waiting to hear the updates from their lives. Some are characteristically quiet on the e-mail updates and some are characteristically … not.

During the big battle at the end of the book, as we were on our way to leaving Iraq, Doc was busy in our final days at Hope dealing with casualties from the NP, the Iraqi Army, and American soldiers. As we left Hope by helicopter to fly back to Baghdad and then back to Fort Riley, Kansas, Doc was submitted for an award for his efforts. A couple of months ago, we got word back that his award was upgraded to an Army Commendation medal with a "V" device for Valor. This is an extremely rare award. Great work, Doc!

Another update I received was about the command sergeant major who controlled all the billeting on the large operating base where we got all of our supplies. She returned to the United States and was court-martialed a few months ago because she was taking bribes to allow individuals or units to live in certain areas on the forward operating base and kicking off others (like us). The situation at the time called for us to vacate our facilities on the base, and she was the reason. It was good to hear that justice was done. She was reduced from a command sergeant major (E9) to a sergeant E5 now, and I heard that she did some confinement time for her actions.

The team is all spread out over most of the United States in various assignments. One left the army. Most of us had some type of follow-on school to complete after Iraq and spent the last few months starting or finishing courses such as Command and General Staff College, the Sergeant's Major Academy, Combined Logistics Captains Course, Military Agents Course, and Pathfinder School, to name a few.

Senator Obama is now president. Soldiers are still preparing for rotations to Iraq. General Petraeus is now the central command commander over Iraq and Afghanistan.

I was speaking to a young lieutenant a few days ago about counterinsurgency and the wars in Iraq and Afghanistan. He had read several books on the subject and was well versed in his history from Vietnam to the present wars. He was adamant about going to Afghanistan and being a military advisor. He asked me why all the captains and senior sergeants smiled a crooked smile when he asked about it.

"Come by my office some time lieutenant," I said, "and I'll explain why we smile."

Index

A

B

C

D

E

F

G

H

I

J

K

S

T

V

W

Y

sb
.23

LaVergne, TN USA
11 August 2010
192910LV00001B/97/P

9 781434 398710